# NORFOLK DOCUMENTS 1
## MR MARTEN'S TRAVELS IN EAST ANGLIA

*Further details of Poppyland Publishing titles can be found at*
*www.poppyland.co.uk*
*where clicking on the 'Support and Resources' button*
*will lead to pages specially compiled to support this title.*

# NORFOLK DOCUMENTS

Norfolk is fortunate in having a wealth of documents surviving from the past millennium. Many are cared for in the Norfolk Record Office at the Archive Centre in Norwich; others remain in private collections. Some documents (and audiovisual materials) are now available online; a few have been published in scholarly editions. However, there remain many fascinating papers known only to specialist researchers. The intent of this NORFOLK DOCUMENTS series is to bring some of these to a wider readership, taking advantage of recent short-run printing technology to present them at reasonable cost for anyone with an interest in East Anglian history.

Instead of being restricted to reproducing what the original author wrote, with all its puzzles of historical reference and sometimes of quirky handwriting, this series includes:

careful transcriptions of the documents;
introductions to set the originals in their historical context;
notes to clarify obscure allusions;
references to further reading;
pictures, either from the original documents or from other sources;
indexing of people, places and themes.

As with all Poppyland Publishing titles from the last few years, further resources and support materials are also being made available on the website **www.poppyland.co.uk**.

Tuesday 13 September

We purposed obtaining permission to mount the top of the elevated Castle in order to have a panoramic view of the City & the Hills which surround it — but we were dissuaded on account of the wind blowing so strong that it would be difficult to stand against it we therefore walk'd round the Castle on the Mount which is lofty enough to afford a view over the Houses & to the distant Hills. Here we counted 23 Steeples of the 36 Churches which the Map of Norwich states to be in it — and prolonged our stay because of the pleasure we enjoyed — There was however some alloy in seeing the Bars and fastnesses preparing for the securing

*A sample page from the Journal held in the Norfolk Record Office (ref. MC 26/1).*

NORFOLK DOCUMENTS 1

# Travels in East Anglia

## The 1825 Journal of Robert Humphrey Marten

Edited by Elizabeth Larby

POPPYLAND PUBLISHING

First published 2012
ISBN 978 0 946148 95 0

Published by Poppyland Publishing, Cromer, NR27 9AN

Designed and typeset in 11 on 14 pt Goudy Old Style by
Watermark, Cromer, NR27 9ER

Printed by Lightning Source

To

Dr Tom James
Professor Emeritus at the University of Winchester

Thanks for the inspiration

# Preface

The *1825 Journal of an Excursion to Yarmouth, Norwich, Cromer, etc* (ref. MC 26/1) is a small handwritten volume that was purchased by the Norfolk Record Office, where it is held, on 1st October 1980. The calfskin-bound diary comprises approximately 130 pages of rather spidery, though on the whole legible, handwriting. An inscription inside the front cover, 'given to Sarah Marten', the diarist's youngest daughter, is in a different hand. At the end of the journal are some rather cryptic notes, concerning flowers, cost of meals, a marriage announcement and an epitaph, that are not reprinted here.

Included in Marten's diary were a plan of Norwich and engravings of Cromer and Yarmouth, as well as seventeen of the diarist's own well-observed line drawings. A map of Norfolk appears to have been torn out of the journal.

Extracts from the journal have previously been published in three articles. The first, by Paul Rutledge, entitled 'Dinner at Earlham', was published in the *Newsletter of the Friends of Earlham* (No. 3, 1981). A further extract appeared in *NARG News* (No. 29, 1982) edited by Norma Virgoe and entitled *A Visit to a Norwich Silk Factory*. Finally, a selection of extracts was published in *Norfolk Fair* (April 1985) under the title 'In Pursuit of Health and Pleasure: An excursion of 1825' edited by Elizabeth Jones. A couple of short extracts and two of the sketches were also published in Christopher Pipe's book *The Story of Cromer Pier* (Poppyland, 1998).

In order to preserve the character of the original text it has been the editorial policy to retain as much of the diarist's spelling, grammar and punctuation as possible. Only for the sake of clarity and consistency have modernisations been made, abbreviations extended and capitalisation altered. All editorial comment within the text, including the page numbers of the diary itself, has been placed in square brackets. At page 83 Marten's numbering appears to go out of sequence, but to avoid confusion this has not been reflected in the text.

To put the journal into the context of its time, further editorial comment, giving details of people, places, and events, has been interspersed with sections of text. The diary has been divided up into seven sections (with titles by the editor) each with notes to explain more specific points or to refer to further sources of information where necessary.

The entries in the journal begin on Wednesday 7th September and end on Friday 30th September, making an excursion of 24 days' duration. The almost daily entries are full of detail and description, but rarely are they of a personal nature: the diarist's companions on his travels, his wife Emma, daughter Sarah, and servant, are barely mentioned. Robert Marten recorded his travels at the age of 62 when all of his five children were grown up and his London business had recently been established. In describing his journey for health and pleasure the diarist has afforded his readers a rare glimpse of the sights and sounds, the characters and happenings of Georgian England.

# Acknowledgements

Many people assisted with my research towards this publication, most of which was carried out over twenty years ago, and thanks are extended to them all. I would also like to thank those who took the time to read and make helpful suggestions about the text. In particular, I am indebted to John W. King, the great great grandson of Robert Marten, who provided me with a typescript of the diarist's autobiography and put right my conjectures over his family tree. I recently discovered a most interesting website www.morganfurman.com which has added greatly to my knowledge about Marten family history.

# Contents

# Illustrations

# Chronological list of events
# in the diarist's life

1763 *21st March* Robert Humphrey Marten born at New Broad Street, Moorfields, London

1776 Engaged as a clerk to work in the London Counting House of Mr Dominique Candide Boyer

1776 Offered a position in the Counting House of Mr Thomas Coles

1782 Experiences a narrow escape from drowning in the Thames

1788 Takes up his Freedom of the City of London and joins the Company of Cooks

1788 Offered a place as book-keeper with Smith & St Barbe, ship brokers

1789 Mother dies

1789 Marries Mary Reeves

1790 Wife dies

1791 Marries Elizabeth Giles

1792 First son Robert Giles born

1793 Becomes a partner in Smith St Barbe & Marten

1793 Daughter Elizabeth born

1794 Son James born

1795 Son James dies

1795 Daughter Mary born

1797 Daughter Mary dies

1797 Son Charles born

1797 Joins Portsoken ward volunteers during civil unrest

1800 Daughter Sarah born

1801 Son George born

1802 Experiences second narrow escape from drowning

1803  Acts on committee of the Patriotic Fund to aid civil defence
1805  Enrols in Regiment of the City Light Horse
1805  Attends Nelson's funeral with regiment
1805  Acts on committee for the relief of German distress
1806  Purchases Broadway House, Plaistow
1807  Gives land for the building of a chapel at Plaistow
1807  Becomes a Life Governor of the London Hospital
1809  Raises money for the relief of famine in Sweden
1809  Becomes a Director of the Kent Water Works Company
1810  Acts on committee opposing Lord Sidmouth's Bill concerning Dissenting teachers
1810  Joins Independent Livery of London
1811  Elected an honorary member of the Royal Humane Society
1811  Second wife dies
1812  Forms a District Bible Society
1813  Marries Emma Martin
1813  Partner, Samuel St Barbe, dies
1813  Raises money for the relief of German distress
1815  Consultation with the Duke of Wellington
1816  Father dies
1816  Appointed Overseer of the Poor for the Parish of West Ham
1816  Presented to Prince Leopold of Saxe Coburgh at Marlborough House
1816  Director of the Commercial Dock Company
1817  Proposes a public meeting to discuss the condition of discharged sailors
1818  Founder of the Port of London Society for Promoting Religion Among Seamen
1819  Nominated for Sheriff of London and Middlesex
1821  Appointed Deputy of the Society for Promoting the Civil and Religious Liberties of Dissenters
1822  Active member of committee to relieve suffering in Ireland
1823  Robert Marten & Sons established in Mincing Lane, London
1824  Director of the Thames Tunnel Company
1825  Tour of East Anglia
1827  Sits on committee for the repeal of the Test & Corporation Acts
1839  *11th December* Robert Humphrey Marten dies aged 76

# Introduction

## The Diarist: Robert Humphrey Marten (1763–1839)

Robert Marten was born on 21st March 1763 at New Broad Street, Moorfields, in London, the second eldest in a typically large family for the period. His father, Nathaniel, a Mile End pastry cook and confectioner, married Martha Clarkson, Robert's mother, in 1759.

In his memoirs Robert wrote of his childhood, recalling in particular the regularity of family prayers. Stating that he was 'borne of pious parents' he gave thanks for the advantage in life of sound religious instruction. Nathaniel Marten was in the habit of attending the Congregationalist (Independent) meeting at Broad Street twice on Sundays and frequently joined another at Devonshire Square in the evenings. Often he would assemble his family and servants and explain in simple terms the principles of Christian faith.

At the age of six or seven Robert was sent away to school at Buckingham with his brother Nathaniel. His education continued at Edmonton and was completed in London. An avid reader, the boy often used his 'play' hours to widen his knowledge, a habit acquired from his father who both read and wrote a great deal. Nathaniel senior was from time to time involved in the religious controversies of the day, and sometimes employed young Robert to copy the manuscripts of his contributions to various journals.

Throughout his autobiography Robert refers to his father in terms of the greatest respect and affection. At times Nathaniel seems more a friend and confidant, at others he is a 'revered parent' and an 'excellent father'. In his father's footsteps Robert later paid his livery subscription to the Company of

Cooks, and became a member of the Broad Street Church where he met his first wife, Mary Reeves.

After assuring himself of her 'pious principles' and sampling her 'sensible conversation', Robert married Thomas Reeves' eldest daughter, Mary, on 18th August 1789 at Bethnal Green. Their wedding day was one of 'very great seriousness' for the bridegroom in the midst of the family celebrations. With his savings of two or three hundred pounds he took a small house in Craven Place and settled down to enjoy 'the peace and pleasantness' of domestic life.

Sadly, the couple's happiness was to be short-lived, for Mary was taken ill during the following year. Despite the benefit of a change of air prescribed by the doctor, a move to Bethnal Green did not bring the hoped-for signs of improvement, and Mary died on 20th June 1790. Robert's sister, another Mary, comforted him following his untimely loss and became his housekeeper and companion. By the end of the year, on the advice of his father, the young man was once again considering marriage.

Having renewed his acquaintance with Miss Elizabeth Giles, a great favourite of his father, Robert proposed and was accepted. He and Elizabeth were married on 12th July 1791 at Milton-next-Gravesend Church. Still living on a very small income, the Martens had to practise economy in the home. No Sunday parties were permitted, for Robert considered these to be unnecessary outlets of expenditure. Instead, the couple lived by the guidelines of a deacon of their church, who advised them to 'work hard, live hard and pray hard', and they remained 'cheerful and thankful' despite their straitened circumstances.

The birth of their first child, Robert Giles, on 22nd June 1792 was an occasion of both joy and sorrow. For the first few days the baby teetered on the verge of death, and at one point his parents almost gave up hope of his survival. The child did live, though, unlike his brother James and sister Mary who both died in infancy. In an age where child mortality was high and families large, the deaths of James and Mary were recorded by their father in his memoirs as simple statements of fact. Robert's brother, Nathaniel, had died 'of a putrid fever' shortly after being sent away to school, and the youngster records that he was 'not so seriously impressed by the event' as his father had feared he might be.

In 1793 improving finances allowed a move to No. 64 Great Prescott Street in London, a comfortable house with a small garden. Robert records that, thanks to the benefits of a new home and daily family prayers, his heart 'rejoiced' in happiness and life took a definite turn for the better.

In the year of his move to Great Prescott Street, Robert commenced work as a partner in the firm of Smith St Barbe & Marten, Ship & Insurance Brokers. The reward of a partnership had finally come after many years of learning the business, and marked a great step forward for the ambitious, now 30-year-old, man. Robert had begun his apprenticeship in London on leaving school with Dominique Candide Boyer, an Italian silk merchant. Once his father had been satisfied that he would not be corrupted through his acquaintance with a Catholic businessman, and on the written agreement that he would never be employed on the Sabbath, Robert was allowed to start work as a clerk in Mr Boyer's counting house. After working for a year without pay, the young man could look forward to a salary of £10 for his second year of service, £20 for the third, and so on until he was earning £40 in his fifth year.

During his clerkship Robert became fluent in Italian, the language used in the counting house, and had high hopes both of a trip to Italy and of furthering his career. Unfortunately, before Robert's five-year contract was due to expire, his employer went bankrupt, forcing the young man to seek new employment. A contract was almost settled with a Mr Maltby of Norwich, when Robert was persuaded by Thomas Coles to work for him transacting the Custom House business of Oswald Godwin & Coles, brokers in general merchandise. Here, he accompanied the partners in the examination of large cargoes of muslins, calicoes, and other goods, and assisted in the outfitting of ships for foreign trade.

Robert appears to have worked hard as a clerk with Oswald Godwin & Coles to establish a reputation for himself. He was obviously seen as being reliable, and recorded that he was treated with 'unbounded confidence' and often entrusted with large sums of money. An opportunity arose for Robert to make a name for himself when he took on and won a legal battle for Mr John Dawson of Liverpool, whose main business was trading in slaves. Working for three years in his spare time in the attics of the Custom House, the young clerk was able to prove that the £600 his client had paid in duty on a captured ship was not legally due. Robert records that he had no idea at the time of the reprehensible nature of Dawson's business, and gratefully accepted a reward of £100 of the amount recovered.

In 1788 Robert discussed his prospects with his employers, not wishing to remain a clerk for too long. Since a partnership looked unlikely, he therefore determined to seek the desired promotion elsewhere. A place as book-keeper at £120 per year with Smith & St Barbe, ship brokers of America Square, was soon obtained, giving Robert new hope of success. At the end of a three-year contract, disappointment resulted once again, however, when Robert was told that he would not, after all, be made a partner. Hurt and insulted by his employers' offer to keep him on as a clerk at any salary he wished to name, he immediately sought work elsewhere. Smith & St Barbe, anxious not to lose a valuable asset, soon reconsidered their decision, and made Robert Marten a partner in the firm in 1793.

His dream finally achieved, Robert records that his fears for the wellbeing of his growing family were allayed, and, with new-found energy and enthusiasm, success crowned his efforts at work. To the firm's main business of insurance, Robert added that of the care and disposal of salvaged ships. During the ensuing wars against France, many captured vessels were consigned to the firm through various naval prize agents and government commissions. Robert's work involved separating 'prizes' from prisoners and dismantling the ships' fixtures and fittings, as well as arranging valuations, surveys, and auctions. On one occasion in 1797, rather uncharacteristically perhaps, he dined in style with Admiral De Winter and his officers on board the *Venerable*, a captured Dutch ship, whilst wounded sailors still suffered below decks.

Business also brought Robert into contact with the influential Levant Company of merchants, dining with them when Nelson was their honoured guest. Through his work for the Independent Livery Company of London Robert was steward at a dinner for 600 people in 1810, and presented a petition to the Prince Regent. He was later introduced to the Prince, who in the next year saw fit to nominate Smith & St Barbe as brokers for detained American property.

While business was proving highly successful the situation at home was not as happy. By 1805, Elizabeth Marten's health was such that she was confined to the house for much of the time, and it was decided that a summer residence in the country where she could regain her strength was desirable. Accordingly, Robert rented a small house in Plaistow, Essex, for £25 per year with his wife's health and happiness in mind. Her brother having recently married a Miss Bevans and settled in Plaistow, it was hoped that Elizabeth's spirits would be lifted by the company of her family.

In the following year a larger residence, Broadway House, was purchased for 2000 guineas. The family finally moved from London and settled in the rural village of Plaistow in 1807, Robert travelling to town each day in his new two-wheeled chaise. A gardener and various servants were added to the now well-to-do household. By 1825, a survey of the parish of West Ham shows that Robert's estate had grown to include a house, yard, garden, and pleasure ground, with an additional garden and orchard nearby.

*Broadway House in Plaistow in the parish of West Ham. It was then a village location a short distance outside London.*

Plaistow in the early nineteenth century had only a small population of 600–1000, but contained several fine houses which were the homes of successful businessmen and wealthy farmers. Broadway House was the largest of these residences, later enlarged and improved by Charles Marten and sold by the family in 1867. By 1878 it is listed in the Post Office Directory as a Home for Destitute Little Girls, but was demolished four years later. The Broadway, on which it stood, was once the hub of the village, where bull-baiting and cockfighting had taken place. National events and political milestones barely affected the lives of the majority of the inhabitants, who were too poor even to afford newspapers. The infamous eighteenth-century highwayman Dick Turpin began his career leading his gang of smugglers between Plaistow and Southend.

On a visit to Plaistow in 1739, John Wesley had been disappointed by a very poor turnout of the faithful to hear his message. Most of the listeners, he said, appeared 'quiet and unconcerned'. When even stronger words failed to move the audience, Wesley concluded, 'it is only the voice of the son of God that can wake the dead!' By the late eighteenth century, the village had acquired a reputation for godlessness, the nearest churches being at East and West Ham.

As more dissenting families moved into the area, however, the need for a suitable place of worship became more pressing.

In 1796, some members of the Independent congregation at Stratford and Bow, concerned at the neglect of the Sabbath at Plaistow, took a room in the village and held services there. Up to 1801, Rev. W. Newman took two services in Plaistow each week, and increasing numbers soon meant that a larger room was needed. It was these later meetings, held in the house of Mr Sparkhall, which Robert and his family first attended when they moved into the village. By 1807 the congregation had once again outgrown its meeting place, and Robert determined to raise the money to build a chapel. A plot of land in North Street was purchased by Robert Marten, John Warmington, Thomas Hagger and John Taylor, and given for the building of a place of worship for Protestant dissenters of both Independent and Baptist denominations.

The new meeting house opened on 15th October 1807, with Robert Marten as one of its founder members and its first deacon, an office he held until his death. The founders of Plaistow's chapel were all businessmen of considerable wealth and social position, and have been described by S. A. Willis in *The Story of Plaistow Congregational Church* as 'men of vision and men of faith'. Instead of ignoring the spiritual and temporal needs of their community, the description goes on, 'they gave liberally of their money, their time, and their talents' not only to establish and run the meeting house, but to serve numerous charitable causes in the area.

Unfortunately, not all of the local inhabitants were as grateful, and from its first day the chapel met with opposition and hostility. Stones were thrown through its windows at night, and even during services. Robert Marten and his family became another target of abuse, and suffered anonymous threatening letters and various other petty annoyances. Opponents tried to start a fair in the village with the specific purpose of annoying 'Marten and his religious crew'. Robert writes in his memoirs of the great fear and anxiety experienced by his family during this trying time, which he says they bore with characteristic patience, believing that ultimately evil would always be overcome by good.

After this unfortunate beginning the chapel thrived and Robert revived and superintended a Sunday School in the village. Ministers from the colleges of Hoxton and Homerton supplied the chapel, and in their absence Marten often conducted the prayer meetings himself. John Burton, a later deacon of the church who knew Robert well, had this to say of its main benefactor:

His kind attentions to the young and to the poor of the flock were unremitting and unwearied, and he was ever watchful to promote the interests of the church, as well as the temporal benefits of all around. He was also distinguished by a large amount of public spirit. Bible Societies, and every effort of religious benevolence found in him a ready advocate and a zealous promoter . . . The village of Plaistow is honoured in having been the abode of such a man, and this church and congregation are no less honoured in having been for so many years the scene of his constant example and his benevolent labours.

Examples of Robert's generosity, both at home and abroad, abound in his memoirs and in the 1825 journal. Helping others was not just a part of his Christian duty, but something in which he obviously took great pleasure. Working on committees to raise money to help those suffering from the effects of wars and famine took up a great part of his free time. Perhaps his greatest effort was in helping to raise £120,000, to which Parliament added £100,000, to aid Germany after the destruction caused by the Napoleonic Wars. This work brought Marten into contact with many rich and powerful figures including the Duke of Wellington and James Monroe, the US President, and won him tokens of respect and gratitude from the kings of Saxony and Prussia and the magistrates of several German towns.

With his friend Luke Howard, Robert was presented to Prince Leopold of Saxe Coburgh, and received thanks for his work in relieving unparalleled distress. Recognition from the burgomaster and senators of Magdeburg came in the Freedom of that city. An honorary membership of the Hamburg Society of Useful Arts and Sciences proved an excuse for Mr Howard to show off his Latin in his letter of thanks. Typically, Robert Marten replied in what he called 'plain and I hope honest English'.

The deplorable condition of sailors discharged from warships prompted efforts of benevolence closer to home. Marten proposed and chaired a public meeting that raised subscriptions towards feeding and clothing sailors in need. A floating hospital was funded out of a surplus of donations. Coming into close contact with distressed sailors gave Robert another opportunity for spreading the word of God, and accordingly he published his ideas on the necessity of making some permanent accommodation for preaching the gospel to the numerous sailors in the port of London. A public meeting followed in 1818 at which Robert Marten became the founder of the Port of London

Society for Promoting Religion Among Seamen. A large ship was fitted out as a chapel and moored on the Thames. In his memoirs Robert writes that both churchmen and dissenters gave willingly to the cause of improving the moral character of seamen, making the project a great success.

In wartime Robert put his organisational talents to good use in one of the many soup societies, helping to distribute cheap and wholesome food to the poor of London. One morning he served 3000 quarts of soup in this capacity. Volunteers also took on the cleaning and whitewashing of slum dwellings in an effort to stop the spread of infectious diseases such as smallpox.

Another, rather unwelcome, opportunity arose to help the needy at home in 1820 when Robert was appointed an Overseer of the Poor for the Parish of West Ham. Coming at a time when he was already overburdened with work, the new post almost stretched its holder to the limits of his patience. Once his wife had pointed out that this could be a good opportunity for making changes and improvements to the system, though, Robert took on his new role with enthusiasm. Religious observance was soon introduced into the local workhouse, along with many other benefits including clean drinking water, all of which, he claimed, produced a marked improvement in the health and welfare of the inmates.

Like many dissenters, Marten was eager to seize every opportunity to spread the faith, distributing religious tracts even whilst on holiday. In 1812 he met with several neighbours in order to form a district Bible Society in South West Essex, and showing typical modesty, he later published a tract he had written himself under the name of the Bible Association.

Marten worked equally hard to spread the message of his sect and to protect the rights of dissenters. In his memoirs Robert records that, with his friend William Phillips and thirteen other gentlemen, he was one of the early subscribers to the London Institution whose aim was to make science available to everyone, in particular dissenters barred from Oxford and Cambridge. In 1811 he formed part of the committee opposing Lord Sidmouth's Bill that aimed to force dissenting teachers to abide by the principles of the Established Church. Hundreds of petitions and considerable public pressure eventually forced the government to withdraw the Bill later that year. Local recognition of Robert's efforts came in 1821, when the congregation at Plaistow elected him as their Deputy for the Society for the Protection of the Civil and Religious Liberties of the Dissenters, on whose committee he later served.

In 1819 Robert experienced one of the many restrictions placed on dissenters for himself when he was nominated for Sheriff of the City of London and

County of Middlesex. As the law required all holders of this position to take the sacrament according to the rites of the Church of England, Robert was in effect ineligible. Finding himself subsequently bound to pay a fine for 'refusing office', Marten complained, alleging that being ineligible he was not liable to pay any fees. He wrote of his reasons for taking a stand on the issue, stating simply that 'this was a matter of right and much concerned the Dissenters'.

Marten's work in supporting various causes brought him into contact with a wide variety of like-minded people, including the charismatic politician and anti-slavery campaigner William Wilberforce, who became a personal friend. Wilberforce visited Plaistow often, and attended chapel with Robert on more than one occasion. When his celebrated book *A Practical View of Christianity* was published, Wilberforce sent a copy to his friend with a flattering testimony inscribed. A grandson of Robert Marten, Dr William Marten Cooke, recalled one of Wilberforce's visits to the family home:

> Here I once saw Mr Wilberforce, who was not an infrequent visitor ... This visit impressed itself the more on my memory because the season had been a very hot and dry one, and I was asked to assist the gardener in watering the lawn (in which my grandfather took much pride) in preparation for the visit.

The image of a grandfather taking pride in his home and garden presents a rather different side of the man of business and the ardent dissenter. Robert was obviously proud of his home and family, and derived great pleasure from domestic life. On the occasion of his youngest son's 21st birthday, the whole family assembled and his children presented Robert with their written thanks for his constant kindness and affection towards them. As a parent, he, in turn, records that he felt indebted to his children's teachers for the 'comfort and honour' the youngsters reflected on him.

On the death of his second wife, Elizabeth, on 6th September 1811, Robert recalls that the years of their union had been 'twenty years of mutual happiness except the interruptions occasioned by personal sufferings of either but these were soothed by sympathy and heightened by mutual affection, she was a tender wife, an affectionate and wise mother and wise councillor'.

Another two years were to pass before Robert found a new partner. Chosen for her very high character, Miss Emma Martin became Robert's third wife on 8th July 1813, and every branch of the family, it seems, 'had reason to rejoice' in the happy event of that day. In a letter to their father in 1822 the now grown-up Marten children referred to Emma as 'your excellent wife, our very affectionate

*Cromer, Norfolk. Engraved by W. Wallis from a drawing by J. S. Cotman for* Excursions through Norfolk (*London: Longman, 1818*)

and valued Mother', whose care and love had amply filled the place of their natural mother.

It was Emma who accompanied Robert on his 1825 tour, and who took every opportunity to aid her husband in his efforts to help those they met who were in need. Whether it be helping a poor widow or a dying man, or contributing towards the education of Cromer children, the Martens' philanthropy and kindness were often in evidence. The thoughtful gesture of presenting a sketch of the Cromer lighthouse to its keeper prompted the following characteristic observation from the diarist:

> How easy it is sometimes by a little costless attention to confer a
> favor and give real pleasure! Then ought we not all to look out for,
> and willingly embrace opportunities where they offer?

On his travels Marten tended to favour places where order, cleanliness and propriety were found. Cromer was praised for displaying such qualities, whilst also having the benefit of regular preaching on the Sabbath to recommend it. Time-wasting was to be avoided, even on holiday, and sketching 'to improve time' often adopted. The Martens appreciated good manners and courtesy, and they were obviously impressed with the civility and respectability of the Cromer folk they encountered. Both the Independent and Baptist sects encouraged high standards of piety and morality, recreational pursuits being discouraged in favour of hard work, sobriety and strict discipline. Moderation in all things was sought, particularly in dress and behaviour, but self-improvement, even financial, provided the money was put to good use, was considered appropriate.

On rare occasions Robert allows his sense of humour to show through the lines of his diary. An embarrassing incident on board ship involving the use of the main cabin as both bedroom and dining room seems to amuse him. Later, an almost irreverent sense of fun is revealed when the tombstone of a Mr Larkins of London is discovered in Cromer churchyard. 'What a memento for travellers!' exclaims the diarist ironically, having just dined at the very inn where the man met his untimely death.

A love of nature and the countryside is also revealed in Robert Marten's diary. As they travelled the couple were curious and alert, taking an interest in all they saw, rivers, wildlife, and seascapes. Robert was particularly impressed to see Thomas Fowell Buxton's collection of wildfowl, which were allowed to roam free and 'unmolested by fear'. In his will the diarist left two cabinets of natural history specimens to his daughter, Sarah, who perhaps shared his interest in the subject, as well as a fine collection of paintings. On holiday, just as we might take photographs, Robert often made sketches to remind him of the views he liked. Sometimes such scenery inspired the poet in him, and he describes in his diary the 'silvery cast of the waning moon on the ripling wave' and the 'mighty boiling cauldron' of the ocean.

Travel featured regularly in Robert's life, both at home and abroad. Some trips were concerned with business, such as that to the Netherlands for ten days in 1802. Others, like the 1825 excursion, were simply for health and pleasure. One particular extravagance was a tour of France in 1818, with a party of six in an English travelling carriage drawn by four horses. Like other curious tourists of their day, the Martens were interested in signs of industrial expansion, displaying in particular a fascination for steam power and its many applications. During their wedding tour, Emma and Robert visited the ironworks at Coalbrookdale and the salt mines at Northwich in Cheshire.

Owing to the vast amount of business and philanthropic work taken on by Robert, he often suffered from headaches and nervous exhaustion, writing that he was in need of a break and some relaxation. This took the form of riding, or playing Hop Ball, a game not dissimilar to cricket. Evenings were spent in the company of his family, and sometimes at dissenters' clubs such as the Highbury Society. Members dined together at an early hour, enjoying conversation of a pleasant and instructive nature, returning home to their families soon after eight o'clock. Often, Robert would organise entertaining and educational lectures for his family and friends at his home on subjects such as music, geography and chemistry.

On 11th December 1839 Robert Marten died of a coronary at his home in Plaistow aged 76. The minute book of the chapel he founded gives a fitting obituary to this large-hearted and well loved character:

> It is our painful duty to record the loss this church has sustained in the death of our highly esteemed brother and deacon, Robert Humphrey Marten Esq. But while we mourn our loss we would not forget the gratitude due to the Great Head of the Church for sparing his valuable life for so protracted a period and rendering him so eminently useful, active and benevolent a member of society in general, and of this church and neighbourhood in particular.

In a sense, Robert Marten mirrors the changing society in which he lived; not only did they share common roots in eighteenth-century England, but both showed symptoms of the great transformation afoot in the nineteenth century. Marten, with his sense of order and tradition, and his preference in all things for the 'solemn grandeur' he observed in Norwich Cathedral, was on one hand the typical eighteenth-century gentleman. Yet, with his interest in the inventions and improvements of his day, his membership of the growing middle class of businessmen, and his role as one of the 'new' dissenters, the diarist was also very much a man of the nineteenth century.

## The Diarist's lifetime

The historical backdrop to the life of Robert Marten and his travel journal is one of change, of a country in transition from a rural to an industrial economy. This 'industrial revolution' has been described as an unprecedented growth of the economy, a massive increase in the output of goods and services. It was far more than this, though, for a 'revolution' was also taking place within society itself.

In 1818 William Howley, Bishop of London, neatly summed up the character of the age, stating, 'It is our lot to have fallen on days of innovation and trouble: the political circumstances of the age have produced an alteration in the circumstance of the country and an agitation in the public mind.'

Notable features of the 'alteration' to which Howley referred were a marked increase in population, the growth of towns, technological inventions, and the development of the factory system. Between 1776 and 1851 the population of England grew from just over seven million to nearly eighteen million.[1] Contemporaries were often astonished by the amount of building under way in towns and cities. Indeed, Marten notes 'a great extension' taking place in Norwich in 1825, and remarks that this was also happening in many other cities.

Looking back in 1898 on *The Wonderful Century* A. R. Wallace claimed 'not only is our century superior to any that have gone before it', but that it was 'the beginning of a new era of human progress'. With her plentiful supplies of iron and coal, as well as a high level of technical skill, Britain became the 'workshop of the world', a leader in industrial development. Steam power was first used industrially in Britain, and the factory system of cotton production appeared as early as 1780–95.

Britain was seen to be 'at the centre of a vast and expanding empire'[2] not only because of her supremacy in industrialisation. For 22 years of Robert Marten's life his country was at war with France and fear of invasion was rife. In 1805 Marten was moved to enrol in a privately funded volunteer civil defence organisation, the Regiment of the City Light Horse. The Napoleonic Wars (1793–1815) ended in triumph for Britain, and a deep sense of national pride naturally arose from victory over a nation with almost three times the population. Wellington returned as a hero to a country of 'new ideas and new movements, impatient of old restraints and intolerant of old privileges and distinctions'.[3]

Despite the massive cost of the wars against France, Britain emerged a richer nation in 1815. Thanks to the stimulus of warfare, export trade had doubled, wages were high and spending power increasing. Lord Dudley exclaimed with confidence and pride, 'I doubt whether any community ever attained such a pitch of prosperity and glory.'

Such national wellbeing was short-lived once the war ended, however. A drop in economic demand, plus the return of over a third of a million men from fighting, soon caused fluctuating prices and unemployment. The National Debt had been substantially increased in recent years to finance the war, and borrowing and high taxation resulted after 1815. The years 1815-22 have been referred to as 'years of disillusion'[4] in economic terms, with cyclical depressions causing hardship and unrest in many areas. In 1825, the year of the Martens' expedition, the City was in the midst of a financial crisis.

The adverse effects of industrialisation were already beginning to be felt in this era. In 1810 it was estimated that one fifth of the population of England and Wales lived in towns of over 10,000 people. By 1851 this had increased to 38%, with poor housing, overcrowding and appalling living conditions being the fate of many who had left the countryside to seek work in the towns. The average working class family of the day was said to suffer from 'not enough space, not enough warmth, not enough light, not enough furniture'.[5] A report of 1842 on the 'Sanitary Conditions of the Labouring Population of Great Britain' stressed an urgent need for improvements in urban areas and brought fears of cholera epidemics spreading out from the slums.

In spite of public health measures to pave streets, build sewers, and install piped water supplies, dirt, disease and squalor were often evident in the industrial towns. In Manchester during the 1820s, half of the children born to working class parents died before reaching the age of five.[6] Patent remedies from 'quack' doctors were all too often the resort of those who could not afford proper medical attention. Even hospitals could be insanitary places, where the dangers of infection were high and mortality rates were thought favourable if they were less than 50%. The Norfolk and Norwich Hospital was one of a number of new establishments which were gradually raising standards, and was praised by an eighteenth-century visitor for being clean and efficient.

Living and working conditions for those employed in the Lancashire cotton industry were particularly bad. An address to Parliament in 1811 warned of the 'frightful situation of that valuable part of the people the Cotton Weavers'. In the following year a Manchester businessman admitted that honest men could not get bread, much less clothes, for their families. Child labour was common in the factories of the early nineteenth century, with children as young as five or six working long hours in damaging environments. In a society where many families relied heavily on the wages of their children, Factory Acts in 1818, 1825, and 1831 to regulate their hours of work were not always a welcome solution.

It has been estimated that as late as 1830 there were still 240,000 handlooms in existence, despite the adoption of steam-powered looms and the introduction of the factory system of cotton production. With increasing competition from cheap, factory-produced cloth, handloom weavers like those encountered by the Martens in Norwich were forced to work longer and longer hours to survive, often in squalid conditions. Opposition to machinery was still commonplace at this time, and handloom weavers who were being forced out of business had much support.

Machine-breaking 'Luddites', the Peterloo Massacre of 1819 and the

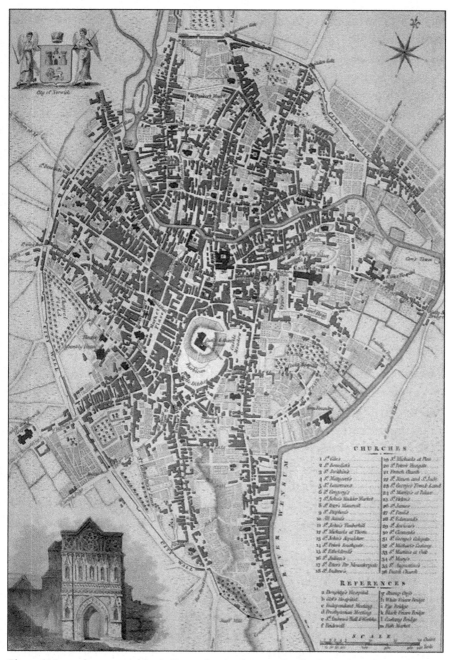

*Plan of Norwich, engraved by J. Roper from a drawing by G. Cole, from Vernor, Hood & Sharpe's British Atlas (1807). The city coat of arms is shown at the top; at the bottom is a view of St Ethelbert's gate below (engraved by J. A. Repton and J. Smith).*

notorious 'Swing Riots' of the 1830s are all extreme examples of the frustrations felt by both people and Parliament at the time. When prices rose and wages fell, as in 1811–12, the result was often violence on the streets, with attacks on both persons and property. Riots, assaults on employers and massive public demonstrations took place after the Napoleonic Wars, just as they had done when the events of the 1789 French Revolution had fired the imagination of the public. Before the days of a state funded police force, Robert Peel's 'Bobbies' being introduced in 1829, private military organisations were often the only means of dealing with such outbreaks. Robert Marten belonged to one such association during the anti-Catholic 'Gordon Riots' of the 1780s, and records in his memoirs the alarm occasioned by the 'infuriated mob'.

The period into which Marten's 1825 diary falls was the beginning of an era of economic growth and relative stability, with both trade and agriculture enjoying a revival. A Conservative government was in power, under Lord Liverpool, from 1812 to 1827, and a new phase of self-reliance and entrepreneurial spirit was in evidence. One contemporary saw Britain 'not merely as shining in arms, or as an emporium of wealth', but 'as a dispenser of blessings to an impoverished world'. The era is often thought of as one in which democracy was nurtured, when humanitarianism began to see the light of day. Many friendly societies were founded in the period 1799 to 1824, providing support to their members in the form of sick pay and other financial benefits. In 1807 the slave trade was abolished, in 1828 the repeal of the Test and Corporation Acts allowed dissenters to sit in Parliament officially, and in 1832 came the Reform Act that allowed the growing middle classes to vote.

As early as 1778 a campaign had begun to improve conditions in British prisons. Elizabeth Fry had embarked on her mission of reform after being shocked by the state of women in Newgate gaol. A 'Society for the Improvement of Prison Discipline' was soon formed, but reforms were only accepted very gradually, with women being placed in the care of female wardresses, and the use of leg irons being restricted to extreme cases. The first prison to put such humanitarian, reforming ideas into practice was that at Millbank, but this remained very much an isolated experiment, one notable exception being the new gaol at Norwich which much impressed the Martens in 1825.

Having won a substantial victory in 1807 over abolishing the trade, the anti-slavery campaign took on a new phase in the 1820s. Anxious to recapture public attention and obtain the release of three quarters of a million black slaves in British Colonies, the campaign used persuasive and impressive moral arguments. Methodist and Baptist ministers brought news of slaves to their congregations, and large amounts of anti-slavery literature helped generate unprecedented support and bring about legislation for the abolition of slavery in British territories in 1833.

Objections to such activities were part of the sweeping rise of 'a powerful humanitarianism which sought, amongst other things, to reform English manners by curbing violence and cruelty'.[7] At home, many campaigned for an end to the blood sports beloved of the gentry. Popular culture such as fairs, rural games and festivals also came under attack, often from members of dissenting sects, and attempts were made to substitute reading rooms, Sunday Schools, and mechanics' institutes in their place.

One group of people sometimes cited as being the catalyst of this humanitarian spirit was the rising middle class. This sector, in which a businessman such as Robert Marten would have fitted, was gradually beginning to play a more significant role in society despite not being given the right to vote until 1832. Many such people worked in the new or expanding manufacturing industries, in banking, commerce, transport or land agencies. Merchants in particular were thriving thanks to British maritime ascendancy and to increasing foreign trade.

Writing of the expanding 'hinterland economies' of growing ports such as London and Bristol, J. Walvin summed up the route to success used by many like Robert Marten: 'It was from these hubs of international commerce', he claimed, 'that so many families of initially moderate means were able to elevate themselves from mere traders into dynasties of opulence and rural property; making that important transition from city traders to country gentlemen'.[8] Purchase of land and setting up a country estate was one way in which this 'nouveau riche' class were improving their social status. Some of these men, like Marten, can be seen as the 'beneficiaries of Britain's expansive overseas empire', the shippers, brokers and colonial officials who had made their way through trade rather than inherited wealth.[9] Often they lived rather precarious lives, with large families to support, with ruin always a possibility.

Much has been written of the link between nonconformists, or dissenters, and success in business. It has been estimated that 49% of the major inventors and innovators in 1811 were dissenters, many of whom belonged to the middle classes.[10] Dissenting attitudes towards work and money have often been cited as a basic cause of such success, hence the warning by Wesley, 'Religion must necessarily produce both industry and frugality, and these can both but produce riches.' Despite such claims, however, it has been suggested that the dissenting academies such as that at Warrington played an important part in the industrialisation process, their intellectual content being favourable to business flair.

The apparent inability of the Church of England to adapt itself to a rapidly changing society produced a wave of 'new dissent' and a steep rise in the registration of chapels from 1790. Whereas complacent Church of England clergy were often isolated both socially and geographically from their congregations, the 'new' dissenters, Baptists, Methodists and Independents, placed great emphasis on evangelism and salvation. In 1833 the dissenters formed a united committee to try to relieve some of their grievances such as the compulsory payment of church rates. Despite the many prejudices against nonconformists, the Victorian era saw the eventual eradication of much of the social discrimination against them.

Religion has been claimed as the driving force behind many of the successful businessmen of the day, including Samuel Morley, Titus Salt and Joseph Rowntree.[11] Characteristics of thrift, hard work, self-improvement and self-discipline were common to many of these nonconformist 'enlightened entrepreneurs'. Another common conviction was that their accumulated wealth should be used for the good of society as a whole. Joseph Rowntree wrote that his aim in life was to combine 'social progress with commercial success'. As employers such men were humane and paternalistic, and in society they showed themselves to share the philanthropic tendencies that Robert Marten reveals in his 1825 diary and his autobiography. Although Marten's dissenting contemporaries were hard workers, they should not, argues I. C. Bradley, be viewed as 'puritanical killjoys'. Many were compassionate, cultivated, and cultured, showing an interest in the arts, education and politics.

George IV, despite being widely distrusted and disliked because of his youthful extravagance and indolence, was said to have provided a 'heart-warming impetus to the art of living'.[12] The monarch, claimed one contemporary, 'seized every opportunity of introducing and encouraging the arts of peace . . . the promotion of religion and morality, the relief of distress . . . never were grander schemes devised for general good than in his reign.' If the early years of the ascendancy of George IV can be said to have been marked by a 'triumph of arms', equally, its conclusion in 1830 was noted for a 'triumph of art'.[13]

The period of George IV's influence is held to be one of the finest for English domestic architecture and interior design. The characteristics of the era were at once a simple elegance and a 'jubilant splendour', its showpieces being Regent's Park and the Brighton Pavilion. Dandies and beaux decorated the social scene, and people took pleasure in eating and drinking, dancing and music. Leisure was diversifying all the time to include race meetings, concerts, theatre, balls and lectures. Cricket, cock-fighting, bull-baiting and boxing were popular forms of entertainment, and the English obsession with placing bets was a constant source of wonder to foreign observers.

A growth of affluence amongst the upper and middle classes meant that more money was available to be spent on leisure and on the all-important country estate, the outward display of taste, wealth and social status. Such residences were often luxurious mansions, filled with Wedgwood china, Hepplewhite furniture, and extensive collections of paintings. The setting was almost as important as the house itself, with formal gardens being replaced by fashionably 'natural' surroundings. This was the era of 'improvements', when those such as 'Capability' Brown and Humphrey Repton tamed the landscape. Exotic foreign plants often appeared in Georgian country estates, along with Greek statues and French and Japanese furnishings.

A cultural revolution was underway, with the spread of ideas and fashions from all over the world encouraging a more civilised lifestyle. Circulating libraries made literature available to the masses, during a period when Romantic poets, letter writers and diarists reached great heights of achievement and popularity. The beginning of the Romantic era saw a rejection of the Age of Reason and rationalism. Poets such as Wordsworth and Coleridge represented a movement encompassing a love of nature and an appeal to the heart rather than the head.

An important catalyst in this social expansion, and in the availability of information, was the revolution in transport that began with improvements to the roads in the eighteenth century. Commercial pressure in this period led to the building of metalled highways, and by the 1830s the turnpike trusts had constructed a network of such roads all over the country. Consequently the period 1760–1860 has been referred to as the 'opening up of England'.[14] The first passenger steamships went into regular service in the early nineteenth century, and continued to operate into the last century, despite enormous competition from the railways from the 1840s.

Travel started becoming easier and cheaper towards the end of the eighteenth century. Both horses and coaches were improved for speed, the post chaise and the stage coach proving the most popular means of travel. In 1801 the London to Brighton journey took 12 hours; in 1830 it took only four and a half hours. Costs were still relatively high, though; in 1774 Parson Woodforde recorded that a journey from Oxford to Somerset cost between ten and fifteen shillings per day, including board and lodgings.

It would appear that during the eighteenth century few people travelled except for business or out of necessity. However, the later Georgian era has been called the first great age of popular travel, when the activity was not restricted to such purposes or to the very rich. From an unpleasant necessity, travel was becoming a pleasure in itself, and even became associated with the idea of an annual holiday. Middle class families were probably able to afford a short yearly holiday, with an occasional trip abroad in emulation of the Grand Tour still favoured by the aristocracy. One contemporary, T. Hurtley, complained in 1786 that 'An universal rage for foreign travel has long occasioned an unaccountable neglect of the beauties of our own country.'

Although travel was becoming comparatively easier and more pleasant, the picture in 1825 was still one of discomfort and often danger, in particular from highwaymen. Coach travel in particular had a rather bad reputation in this respect. Vehicles sometimes overturned, or got stuck in the mud, they usually left at unsocial hours, and it was not unknown for passengers to die from exposure if seated outside a coach in winter! One man walked from Devon to London 'in preference to the purgatory of being for three days sealed up in the jolting and rumbling machine.' A more seasoned traveller, John Byng, wrote of one coach journey where 'we sulked along in much heat and inconvenience . . . I could neither stir, or breathe, or see out of the windows'. However, despite such an experience, Byng concluded in 1794 that 'even under this comparatively miserable system, how superior was England, as a land for the traveller, to all the rest of the world'.

Some inns, such as that encountered by the Martens in Cromer, provided a good standard of accommodation and service, but others were appalling. John Byng concluded that 'The imposition in travelling is abominable', reporting that 'the innkeepers are insolent, the hostlers are sulky, the chambermaids are pert, and the waiters are impertinent; the meat is tough, the wine is foul, the beer is hard, the sheets are wet, the linen is dirty, and the knives are never clean'd.' Towards the end of the era, as the Martens discovered, standards had improved considerably.

As early as the seventeenth century a few people had begun to travel to observe antiquities and curiosities of nature. John Byng was a typical antiquarian, seeking out ruins and castles with an almost religious zeal, his stated purpose being to compare the ancient structures with the fashions of his own day. It has been claimed that, so great was the need to make such discoveries, where none existed they were imagined, as in Thomas Pennant's description of the Yorkshire hills as 'an aggregate of Druidical antiquities'.

Not only did the eager Georgian traveller hunt ruins, he also sought out the 'picturesque' in terms of landscape. The clergyman William Gilpin has been credited with laying down the rules of scenery-spotting in the 1770s in publications such as *Observations on the River Wye*. Landscape came to be treated in much the same way as painting, requiring balance, contrast, proportion as well as a sense of wildness to be worth looking at, explaining the popularity of Wales and the Lake District at this time. Marten was no exception to his contemporaries, often seeking out the picturesque view, despite E. D. Clarke's contention in 1790 that 'the world is weary of that word picturesque'.

Even though travel was gradually becoming associated with the idea of an annual holiday, it was often still linked with health. Following Dr Russell's claims for the benefits of seawater in the 1750s, there had been a move away from the inland spas to the seaside towns. Resorts such as Scarborough attempted to recreate the select atmosphere of the spas with reading rooms and visitors' lists. Royal patronage of Weymouth and Brighton helped to boost the popularity of the seaside.

It has been argued that as early as the 1760s the structure of modern travel was already beginning to come into existence. Maps and guidebooks were only a part of a great surge of illustrated material relating to travel in Great Britain. Dr Granville, the 'first professional travel journalist', wrote of his travels around the coastal resorts in an age where books on travel were the bestsellers. By 1825, travel had become an important part of the social calendar. It was considered so unfashionable to spend all year in London that people even shut up their houses and pretended to be away if they could not actually afford a holiday.

Travel writing had become a sufficiently popular activity by 1812 to attract the pen of the satirist. In *The Tour of Dr Syntax* the diarist rushes to a publisher with his account, only to be greeted with the following ditty:

> Tour, indeed! – I've had enough
> Of Tours, and such-like flimsy stuff.
> What a fool's errand you have made
> (I speak the language of the trade),
> To travel all the country o'er,
> And write what has been writ before.

By the end of the eighteenth century almost the whole of Britain had been visited and described by the tourist. The early Georgian traveller saw himself as an explorer visiting untamed lands; it was his duty to describe all he saw in minute detail to benefit those who might follow in his footsteps.

Regional differences appear very marked in such literature, and as James Boswell remarked to Dr Johnson whilst visiting Scotland, 'it was much the same as being with a tribe of Indians'. Thomas Pennant was one of the first to admit to travelling in his own country purely for pleasure. His obituary in the *Annual Register* of 1804 gives an amusing insight into the attitudes of Georgian people towards their own country: 'He published an account of his journey [to Scotland]) which proved that the northern parts of Great Britain might be visited with safety, and even with pleasure.'

Many Georgian travellers claimed that they did so out of curiosity and to be morally uplifted by seeing how those of a higher class lived. This 'universal curiosity' is a striking feature of the emerging genre of travel literature, with everything being considered noteworthy, scenery, people and industry. Factories, mills and mines, the evidence of a changing landscape, were visited with enthusiasm, and the processes of new technology recorded with accuracy and often in painstaking detail.

In many respects, Robert Marten's 1825 journal is typical of the literature of travel written in the Georgian era. His matter of fact, guidebook style is one that can be found in many other contemporary journals. T. R. Malthus' *Scottish Holiday* of 1826 and M. Gray's *Tour in the Isle of Man* of 1822 are both highly comparable. The latter is similarly a journey undertaken for health and pleasure, and the following comment by its author might equally be applied to the Marten diary: 'Our daily employments have much sameness about them'. An endless round of ruins, churches, country seats, walks and sketching was common, it seems, to most Georgian holidays, but such accounts are fascinating to us for they serve as a snapshot of a very different age to our own.

# 1825 Journal

of an excursion to Yarmouth, Norwich,
Cromer, etc., etc.

# 1

# London to Great Yarmouth

## All aboard the *Hero* steamship
## for adventures on the high seas

Wednesday the 7 September 1825

Embarked at 7 in the Evening at Custom House lower stairs on board the Hero Steam Packet of 350 Tons, carpenters measurements 242 Register[1] – the difference being abated for the Room in which are her two Engines each of [blank] Horses power – and bound for North Yarmouth – My Wife & Daughter accompanying me and our servant attending us – The usual bustle with watermen, wherries[2] etc. at the stairs.

A Steam Packet arrived while we were waiting and added another to the many noble vessels of this description now riding – or departing or arriving at moorings off the Custom House and the Tower. What an entire[ly] new scene this from any thing know[n] only ten [2] years since. I remember but a few months since going to the Riverside to see a Vessel moved rapidly by Steam as a novelty, & much interested was I, & ten thousand more; and now, a Steam-going Vessel is no more a wonder than is a London Wherry on the Thames. Steam Vessels, now, go from London to Margate, Ramsgate, Yarmouth, Scarbro [Scarborough], Leith, etc., etc., regularly at fixed hours like Stage-Coaches, and go, also, foreign to Hambro [Hamburg], Ostend, Rotterdam, Calais, Boulogne, Dieppe, Bordeaux, Gibraltar, Meditteranean, etc., etc. One of upwards of 500 tons has already departed full of passengers for <u>Calcutta</u>!!! Whereunto this will grow future generations may declare [3] but the present race of men are hardly competent even to conjecture.

The Marten family's journey starts from the London Custom House where shipping dues or taxes were collected. This was a building well known to the diarist, whose work in ship insurance often took him there. The first Custom House had been built by John Churchman in 1382, but was burnt down in the reign of Elizabeth I. Subsequent Custom Houses suffered the same fate. The building mentioned here was constructed between 1815 and 1817.

The excursion begins with a voyage on the *Hero* steam packet built at Deptford in 1821, owned at this time by the General Steam Navigation Company. The two engines to which the diarist refers were made by Boulton and Watt.

As such vessels were the first to travel steadily and with reasonable speed to their destinations, steam packets were said to have 'marked the very beginnings of modern travel'.[3] A great advance had occurred in 1815 when steam packets made the trip from London to Margate in eight hours. As the diarist records, in 1825 the *Enterprise* travelled from Falmouth to Calcutta. The journey took 113 days under sail and steam. In the same year the opening of the Stockton to Darlington Railway effectively spelled the end of the Georgian era of travel.

Such thoughts naturally suggested themselves while pacing the deck, waiting 'till we should hear the tide-bell at Billingsgate announce the High-Water – as we were expected to sail with the earliest of the Ebb.

Often thoughts were almost necessarily suggested on viewing the ruins of the Custom-House, recently built at an expense of nearly, if not exceeding, £750,000!, and which for want of a solid foundation had sunk beneath its own weight, & whose centre had already been pulled down. It shewed a melancholy frustration of human expectations. How I pity the architect who has gloried in his fancied permanent elevation! which, like the pride which he thought himself warranted in indulging [4], has eventually been levelled with the dust; leaving, in its stead, a stigma which will not be worn out while himself is an Inhabitant of the World in the praise of whose Inhabitants he had flattered himself with a lasting renown.

After only a few years the new Custom House building showed signs of decay, and in January 1825 the entire central section had been demolished. Ironically, in the light of Marten's remarks, the architect David Laing (1774–1856) was forced to retire in the wake of the litigation following this disaster, suffering extreme financial distress. Sir Robert Smirke (1781–1867) was responsible for building the impressive new river frontage of Portland stone that was nearly 500 feet long.

**It was not quite beside the subject to think for a moment on the importance of the tried solidity of Bases in other things more durable than any in this fleeting state. That Foundation which is designated as the "tried Corner Stone"[4] came to the mind of the writer; & a building thereon in preference to any sandy foundation seemed in his view, on the melancholy scenery there before his Eyes, as of paramount value.**

**[5] The Lights shining on the Noble Bridge of London, there, so near; and the utility of a communication in which Art had triumphed over nature for the convenience of the almost unnumbered Inhabitants of London, gave birth to thoughts relating to the extent of human intellect. These extended to the novel undertaking of the Tunnel, then constructing beneath the bed of the Noble Thames! – an undertaking to which the most scientific, natives and foreigners, paid great homage, and who looking to it with silent admiration, awaited the results in confidence of success:- and led further, rising from the works of human intellect to the Great Source of wisdom, to praise Him from whom every great design, as well [as] [6] every good work proceeds.**

Here Marten describes the sights of the Upper Pool of London, once one of the busiest parts of the Thames. He refers to the new London Bridge, designed by John Rennie, whose first stone had been laid on 15th June 1825. When this bridge was finally opened in August 1831 the old one had been demolished. Another great building venture of the same year was the Thames Tunnel, linking Wapping and Rotherhithe. Marten had been made a director of the Thames Tunnel Company in 1824, and naturally took an interest in its progress in passing. Built by Sir Marc Isambard Brunel (1769–1849) this, the very first tunnel beneath the Thames, took 20 years to complete and cost many lives. Work on the tunnel, nicknamed 'The Great Bore', progressed slowly, at just over two feet per week, eventually being opened in 1843. The Thames Tunnel was finally sold to the East London Railway and became part of the underground network.

**Soon after the Tide-Bell at Billingsgate had ceased, there were evident**

preparations made for departure. Long previously to this the Engineers, Fire Stokers, etc., etc., had been busy in getting the fire in greater ardency, and the Steam more up, to be ready for the command to <u>go on</u>. Essays had been made on both Engines to see that they were in <u>Gear</u> so that when the word should be given there should be no disappointment.

In these trials it was to a novice – (which the writer owns himself to have been in no small degree) – most wonderful to perceive how absolutely this amazing force by Steam is held under control. The Commands to <u>go on</u>: [7] to <u>Stop</u>: <u>Ease her</u>: <u>go gently</u>: <u>very gently</u>: <u>back her!</u>: <u>give her gentle slow way</u>: <u>go on</u>: – etc., etc., were as readily fulfilled as would have been Commands from a superior officer to the best disciplined Regiment in the British Army.

With such obedient forces the skilful pilot threaded his way through the Ships in London's crowded harbor, safely, and without touching the numerous vessels which he had to pass.

We started at about half past nine o'clock. The night was starlight, & clear. The Lamps at the entrance to the London Dock pointed out the access to that noble, and beneficial aid to the Commerce in the Thames. While those at the Commercial Docks, and other important [8] auxilliaries to the Metropolitan Trade challenged our attention <u>en passant</u>.

Situated immediately east of the Tower of London were the London Docks, opened in 1805 and used by vessels in the short sea trade and on coastal routes. The docks were closed in 1968 having proved uneconomic. The Surrey Commercial Dock, two miles below London Bridge on the south bank, had been in operation since 1676. At one time Marten was a director of the Commercial Dock Company.

No doubt the diarist had other, more unpleasant, memories of this area, for in 1802 he had narrowly escaped drowning there. After visiting several ships in the Pool on business, Marten and his companion had been run down by a barge. Robert, who could not swim, was swept beneath the barge and feared for his life. This frightening experience left him in a highly agitated state of mind and prevented him from sleeping for several months. He was later made an honorary member of the Royal Humane Society, a charity that rewards the saving of human life, for services rendered.

The lights of Greenwich Hospital elicited conversation on British gratitude to Britain's naval Defenders; and the Works at Blackwall, and the large

Steam Vessels there for the communication between London and Edinburgh, shewed the spirit of British Enterprise, and led to hope that such facility of intercourse would result in a strengthened Bond of national unity.

Woolwich and its immense arsenal for public defense, and the employment of delinquents for the public weal[5] while at general cost, were worthy of the observations [9] which they elicited while walking the long deck of the handsome <u>Hero</u> in which we were safely proceeding on our excursion for health and for pleasure – the latter essentially contributing to the former.

The diarist makes reference to the naval hospital at Greenwich, and typically uses it for a call to patriotism. The hospital had been built in 1698, and by 1814 it was home to 3000 seamen and also gave out alms to 32 'out pensioners'. Complaints about the food and the harsh discipline plagued the hospital. The custom of making the sailors wear their yellow-lined coats inside out as a punishment led to their nickname 'canaries'.

A contemporary of the diarist, Louis Simond (1767–1831), remarked on Greenwich Hospital: 'It is a beautiful edifice, singularly disposed . . . it is not only the most magnificent of hospitals, but the most cheerful I ever saw. It does not prevent, however, the old sailors who inhabit it from looking very tired and melancholy'.

Marten's reference to the 'Works' at Blackwall is possibly to the notable shipbuilding going on in this area, the Blackwall Tunnel not being built until much later. The Royal Arsenal, originally known as the Royal Warren, can be dated back to at least 1701, the date of the earliest surviving plan. It was used for the manufacture and testing of arms for many generations. A Royal Military Academy had been established nearby since 1741, and a foundry from the 1770s.

In the great Cabin some of the Passengers took tea, others grog,[6] & some partook of wine! The Steward, mean while, prepared the sofas, and the Soft Matresses for Midnight reclining; and the <u>Stewardess</u> was busy with her arrangements in the Ladies cabin for <u>their</u> night repose.

By the Ghostlike hour of 12 many had wrapt themselves in their Blankets or other night attire, and were lost in sleep, or were seeking soft slumbers' pleasing oblivion, but some more sturdy still paced the Deck in [10] the expectation of seeing the silvery cast of the waning moon on the ripling wave.

Our passengers were about 25 and would pay about £21 for Passage Money at 20s. best cabin & 15s. servants. We had according to my calculation about 25 Tons Goods at 6d. foot or £20 to £25 [?freight]. A Voyage to & fro at best might make £90 to £100 per week. This may pay the coals & Wear & Tear and servants wages & interests of Capital & Lights & pilotage and a variety of Contingencies yet we could not form any sanguine expectation of encouraging profit to the Owners.

It is interesting that the diarist, with his knowledge of shipping and business, questions the economic viability of the *Hero*. It has been claimed that only a vessel of around a thousand tons would have enough 'saleable' space to be assured of making a profit.[7]

[11] I rested but slept very little, and when about 5 in the morning I saw day light & peeped through the window near my head I saw the green sea on a level with my nose & running calmly and quietly altho' a little frothily from the motion of the Wheels which worked at no great distance from my resting place.

At the invitation of returning day I left my Couch and on reaching the Deck saw the Shears[8] beacon on the Essex coast. A little rain had fallen and the deck was wet. The clouds were breaking to Windward. To leeward[9] the sky was very heavy. The whole gradually cleared away and by 6 o'clock when breakfast was announced we had chearful weather and lively countenances around our table.

[12] The Breakfast (at 1/6 each) was of Tea or Coffee, Ham, Beef, Eggs, Bread, Butter, etc., etc., & all good of their kind.

As this was in the great cabin which had been used as a Bedroom and the hour was early one of our Friends had not risen – and as he proposed rising while breakfast was proceeding – his Wife who had risen before him very delicately left the table and held a Blanket to screen the whole scenery until [he was] better adapted to public notice.

When breakfast was over & a little time had been allowed for the toilet the Passengers appeared in comfortable spirits on the Deck. A spacious room for promenade on the deck was occupied by many [13] of them and conversations followed with the little platoons into which the society soon fell.

I had the pleasure of the free communication with Major B. of the Marines

– the inventor of the useful Lock Covering for Muskets by which our Soldiers were enabled in the Peninsula to load and fire altho' the heaviest rain fell on them & which quite incapacitated their opponents – and also of a new method of loading great Guns without the usual process of Springing, Ramming, etc. – Mrs. Marten found Mrs. B. equally a pleasant companion & thus occasionally joining conversations & occasionally separating into parties we found the Morning went fast & chearfully away.

Conversation with Major Bartleman continues the theme of national pride, in this instance concerning the Peninsula Wars (1808-14) fought against the French in Spain and Portugal. John Bartleman was commissioned as 2nd Lieutenant in the Royal Marines in 1793. He became a major in the army in 1813, and was transferred to Woolwich in 1825. As noted here by Marten, and reported in the 1811 *Globe and Laurel*, Bartleman was responsible for the invention of a musket lock cover. This device was said to possess 'advantages superior to anything of the kind hitherto adopted', and 40,000 were sent out to Portugal for use in the field against the French armies.

**Mrs. M. found another person [14] whose circumstances appeared to invite those attentions which she never denied when she could think them likely to be beneficial. She had remarked a lady attentive to a Gentleman who appeared much out of health & she asked particulars. The Gent. was her husband – a Capt. S. who had been long ill of Rheumatic Fever & who began to think that he should never recover. He was beside this very low because his hope as to another state was so languid as to scarce deserve the name. She therefore spoke to him on the subject of health of both body and soul & I have hope that her conversation may have a blessed effect.**

**The servant of Major B. having [15] informed him of the very peculiar circumstances of a poor young widow in the fore-cabin Mrs. M. went to her. She was the mother of three children, two of whom had died – the Husband had caught the infection of which he sickened on arrival in London – videlicit[10] of the Small Pox – and was dead before she could reach to see him. She was returning with her only child, and being known to the Captain her passage and food were given to her.**

Deaths from rheumatic fever have been drastically reduced in Britain, due to social as well as medical reasons: better housing, less overcrowding, public health measures. Smallpox has been eliminated now, but in 1825 the practice of inoculation against the disease was not yet widespread. The ravages of smallpox only began to lessen in the 1840s when safer methods of vaccination were introduced and initial public opposition had been overcome. A contemporary of the diarist, William Mavor (1758–1837), referred to smallpox as 'that great scourge of the age' and expressed his regret that vaccination was not recommended by every public and private authority.

As we continued near the Coast varying our distances according to the Bays & Headlands from three to perhaps nine or ten miles we had a fresh succession of objects in the Towns and Forts and Light-Houses on our [16] Larboard[11] hand, while Vessels near and distant attracted notice on our Starboard side. On the former we had Walton,[12] Harwich, Landguard,[13] Orford, Aldborough, Leystone [Leiston], Dunwich, Southwold, & Lowestofte with its many herring vessels ready for launching. The Albion Steamer passed us from Yarmouth bound to London.

We had during the morning a sudden alarm from an accident to the Starboard Wheel. The Balls or Rivets of one of the Iron plates had worked loose & permitted the plate to fly partly off. This, with the velocity & power of the Wheel came in contact [17] with the upper part of the Paddle Box, the Boards of which were instantly torn away & were driven in various directions. The Engine was ordered to be stopped: the Engineers & even the Stokers came in a throng hurrying to enquire the cause of the clatter. The Passengers – especially the females soon imagined a calamitous blow up & more than danger [to] follow – but the cause being quickly ascertained – the remedy was immediately applied – and in ten minutes we were again on our Voyage as if no interruption had taken place.

An early breakfast – a Sea Air & a good walk on the Hero's long deck had led to some enquiry as to the hour for dinner – and from these causes One o'clock seemed to arrive but slowly.

[18] But at 1 we had a fine Leg of Mutton boiled – a piece of Beef roasted & a cold joint of salted boiled Beef – with plenty of good vegetables all well cooked and neatly served & with succeeding pastry at 2/6 each – Ale, Wine etc., were charged separately. Mrs. Bartleman noticed our comforts and proposed remembering the afflicted widow whose whole remaining pecuniary stock was the miserable amount of 1/6. Everyone at Table contributed & Mr. Squires obligingly carried the paper round on the Deck. The Widow, on receiving the subscription of Two Sovereigns, replied only by tears the effect [19] of a grateful heart & in that simplicity which real

suffering unexpectedly allieviated could, alone, display. The appeal was felt
by her benefactors and replied to by a silent expression of feeling – more
affecting than by the eloquence of the most chosen words.

Early nineteenth-century travel was beset with dangers, as many of the
accounts testify. These were still experimental years for steam travel, and the
early steamships seem to have been particularly prone to accidents. The service
between Yarmouth and Norwich, for example, was discontinued for some
years following the panic occasioned by the bursting of the boiler of one vessel
immediately after she had set out.

# 2

# Great Yarmouth

## Seaside, ships and steamers

While this gratifying scene was concluding the Hero entered the River Yare & proceeded to the entrance of the Town of Yarmouth passing Gorleston & Southtow[n] on the right Bank and which are in the county of Suffolk.[1]

We landed at ¼ past 2 having been 17 hours on our passage from the Custom House London.

With Major & Mrs Bartleman we took up our quarters at the [20] Crown and Anchor Tavern on the quay and near the Bridge.[2]

After their long journey the Marten family must have been relieved to reach Great Yarmouth and find their chosen accommodation. The Crown and Anchor Tavern, called at various times 'The Mitre' and 'The Sun', had been partially rebuilt and cased in white bricks in 1811. Unfortunately the diarist does not give us his opinions of the comforts of the inn, but the following lines from a humorous poem of 1822 provide a contemporary's point of view.

> Excerpt from Dr Sigma's poem *A Tour in Pursuit of Ideas (Being a picturesque view of all the Yarmouth Public Houses)*
>
> As when some warrior from the field return'd,
> Crown'd with the laurels he has dearly earn'd;
> Is by his prince and country welcomed home;

So to the Crown and Anchor Inn I come;
Met by the landlord A....n T.......r[3] polite,
I crack my bottle like a tourist bright;
Look o'er the papers and enquire the news,
Collect my thoughts, and thus myself amuse;
Think on my toils in traversing the town,
Note all the incidents, and put them down,
Converse with company and merchants there,
Free from fatigue, perplexities, and care.
O envied state! and hospitable inn,
For situation eligibly fine!

As we proceeded thither we admired the pleasantness of the Town – the number of ships in the Harbor, – the goodness of the Houses & the apparent general order & neatness of the Place.

We had an Evening walk on the fine Jetty extending far into the sea and to which we walked over the fine sands on the shore almost more than shoe deep & which made walking a matter of considerable labor.

The fatigue & want of our usual night-comfort made an early retreat to our Beds very [21] desirable and we were not long before we had wholly forgot the pleasures and the fatigues since our early rising.

*Yarmouth bridge. This and the pictures on pages 50, 52 and 54 were engraved by Joseph Lambert and published in* Graphic Illustrations of Great Yarmouth and its Environs *(1822).*

*Yarmouth Roads and pier.*

The Martens were certainly not alone in their admiration for the charms of Yarmouth. In 1714 Daniel Defoe had credited the town with having 'the finest quay in England, if not in Europe'. William Cobbett received a 'hearty welcome' in 1821, and left with 'the sincerest regard' for all he met. An early Georgian guidebook pronounced Yarmouth to be 'excellently paved, well lighted, and kept uncommonly neat and clean'. Although unimpressed with the surrounding flat countryside, a visitor of 1827 considered Yarmouth superior to Norwich in terms of its buildings and streets, and later predicted, 'In a few years Yarmouth will be the most enviable watering place of any on this coast.'

Yarmouth had had a jetty for landing goods and passengers from ships moored in the Roads, or anchorages, since the sixteenth century. The Marten family enjoyed a stroll on the new jetty, or pier, built in 1808 at a cost of £5,000. This impressive structure was 450 feet long and 20 feet wide, and soon proved popular with the town's growing numbers of summer visitors. The Wellington Pier, one of the first pleasure piers in the country, was built in 1853 in response to this popularity, and was followed by the Britannia in 1858.

### Friday 9 September

**We breakfasted en famille with the Major and his Lady & I then accompanied them to the Jetty where the Boat which the Major had engaged was prepared. They got into it on the Beach and were launched through the surf by the united strength of many stout men. They had four seamen in the Boat – & when round the Jetty head set their Main and Mizen Lug sails[4] & went away for Mund[e]sley with a side wind blowing a pleasant breeze. This conveyed them [22] thither about 30 miles in three hours and twenty minutes: and for only 24/- the Major, his Lady, their servant, two Pointers & all their Luggage were without trouble to them conveyed that distance.**

Taking visitors on boat trips must have provided useful additional income for a community that had been dependent on fishing since the eleventh century. During the seventeenth century the town was still the most important fishing port in England, and in the nineteenth, the fishing industry in Yarmouth was enjoying its greatest expansion. An account of 1817 states that out of the three towns of Yarmouth, Cromer and Mundesley, who shared 150 boats and employed 1,200 men, Yarmouth had by far the largest catch. Particularly important were the prolific herring and mackerel fisheries that were said to have been the foundation of the town's prosperity. Pigot's Directory, c. 1830, comments that Yarmouth crews 'rank amongst the most expert seamen on the British coasts'.

*Norfolk naval column in memory of Horatio Lord Nelson.*

The Master of the Tavern procured for us the loan of the Boat of the William Tell Brig of about 80 Tons & with two nice young Lads for Rowers we went down the River with the Ebb - surveying the shipping from the very bridge - & noticing the 16 ships building - one of which is to be launched tomorrow. We saw the Hero repairing her Paddle Box & having passed South[t]own we landed [23] at Gorleston near the Yare's mouth. Somewhat beyond Gorleston (which is in Suffolk - the Yare dividing the Counties here) there are heights of much verdure affording a distant view over the Land and along the Coast to the westward & a wide expanse of sea. Here we sat for some time enjoying the sight of a Young party seated & taking their refreshments: the ships and Boats under sail & at anchor - those nearer within the long Pier and up the River - the Pillar erected on Yare-mouth Denes in memory of the gallant Nelson - the Jetty,[5] and the distant town of Yarmouth with the numerous Ships in the Roads, the more distant then getting [24] under weigh on the turning of the Tide.

On their trip down the river Yare the Marten family are quick to note the flourishing shipbuilding industry for which Yarmouth was renowned. The town had a reputation for strength and excellence of construction in this field that dated back to the Middle Ages. John Preston stated in his *The Picture of Yarmouth* (1819) that 'in general Yarmouth built ships stand deservedly high in the estimation of the mercantile world'. Many ships used in the Napoleonic Wars were built in Yarmouth, and by 1819 the town boasted eight shipbuilding yards, and produced between 30 and 40 vessels a year. In 1818, a year of unprecedented demand, 100 ships were built and launched from Yarmouth.

Having landed at Gorleston, once described as the 'aristocratic suburb of Yarmouth',[6] the family are treated to excellent views from the cliff tops. Yarmouth's commons, or 'Denes', have been used for many purposes, from drying nets and grazing cattle to defence. Horse racing had taken place on the South Denes from the eighteenth century onwards, and the town's corn mills and gallows were there also. By 1825 the Denes had begun to be developed in connection with the growing holiday industry, and many new houses had been built there.

The diarist must have been particularly gratified to see the memorial to Nelson on the South Denes, as he had once dined with the 'Norfolk Hero', and also attended his funeral. In 1800, on returning to England after the Battle of the Nile, Nelson was given the Freedom of the Boroughs of Yarmouth and Norwich, to which he responded with the words, 'I am myself a Norfolk man

*Yarmouth jetty*

and glory in being so'. After Nelson's death, in 1805, it was decided to erect a monument in his honour. The 'Norfolk Pillar', a 144-foot (44 m) tall column, was completed in 1819 and stands both as a memorial and a seamark. Designed by the Norfolk-born architect William Wilkins, the column, complete with gilt statue of Britannia, predates that in Trafalgar Square. Supposedly, Dickens visited the Nelson memorial and modelled his character Ham Peggoty in *David Copperfield* on the caretaker there, one James Sharman.

The Pier is a fine long walk, well taken care of, & is an inviting promenade, having nothing in the way of the pedestrian to whom the sea view is well open & under whose Eye the <u>Fishers</u> – Men & Boys – sit on a lower part – are watching their floats or occasionally drawing up their little captives. On the Pier we found a family sitting on some timber. They were in deep mourning and there was something so peculiarly sad and mournful – so dejected & solitary in their appearance – that our notice was almost involuntarily fixed on their manifest heavy sorrow.

[25] We thought Gorleston a very quiet & pleasant retreat for those who in their recreation would prefer abstraction from the bustle of business – while from the circumstance of this being the outlet & inlet for all numerous Ships of Yarmouth, every tide must present sufficient novelty to remove from fear of overmuch solitude.

We left our Lads the tract of the Dairyman's Daughter for their amusement while we walked & we almost surprised them on our return so much were they still taken with the History which we found them reading.

The distribution of religious tracts was a common trait of nineteenth century dissenters like the Martens. The story of the Dairyman's Daughter, which the diarist left for the young fishermen, was one of the most famous of the period. *The Tale of the last illness of the Dairyman's Daughter and her demise in an odour of sanctity* was the work of Rev. Legh Richmond (1772–1827) and first appeared in a periodical in 1811. The tract was later circulated in vast numbers and even translated into several languages.

On our return up the River we met the large "Waterloo" Steam Packet belonging to the "General Steam Navigation Company" [7] & was bound for London, fare 20/- each [26] In the Evening we walked through Regent Street & Chapel Street,[8] both well paved & with flagged footpaths, and have very good & handsome Houses. Mrs M. paid her promised visits to the Widow,

*The market place, Great Yarmouth, engraved by John Preston and published in* The Picture of Yarmouth *(1819).*

and to Captain S. and joined us for an Evening's walk on the long Jetty, then the promenade of, as we estimated, about 200 persons enjoying the Sea-Breeze and the lively & pleasing Sea View.

Once it had been established that sea bathing was not only a safe, but actually a healthy pursuit, resorts such as Yarmouth began to enjoy increasing popularity with the holidaymaker. By 1819 the town was becoming well equipped for its annual visitors, with a jetty, bathhouse, bathing machines and souvenirs. John Preston confirms that 'From the beginning of June to the middle of October Yarmouth is much resorted to by families of gentility of Norfolk and Suffolk, as well as from London, and other parts of the kingdom, and it abounds with convenient and elegant lodgings.' By 1836, William White in his Directory was commenting on Yarmouth's 'great celebrity as a bathing place'.

### Saturday 10 September

We rose early and went to view the Market Scenery which here is busy, and very extensive, for Provisions, Vegetables, Fruit, Flowers, [27] Butter, Honey-Comb, etc., etc., and at 9 O'clock went on board a Steam Vessel of 2-6 Horse power Engine bound for Norwich. It was just at this hour Highwater: the Weather fair, sun clear, & every thing inviting & except that the Country being flat, and the River having extensive flat sides which had been & were still overflowed, the wind which blew strongly, felt cold.

The local market was another attraction for early visitors to Yarmouth. Somewhat later, in 1880, the *Chelmsford Chronicle* declared Yarmouth's market to be the best in East Anglia, and claimed that at Norwich to be 'very inferior to it, both for the extent of space occupied and the quality of the provisions on sale'.

The Yare soon divided, & one branch went more to the Northward part of the Country: & another branch went off toward Bungay & is called the Bungay River.[9] Wild Fowl were passing us over-head, & some flew from the River as our approach disturbed [them]: & a Heron rose from the Bank very [28] near to us. Many large Sailing Boats (called here Wherries)[10] well covered by their Hatches, & deeply laden, passed, or were passed by us, as we ascended this very winding & pretty river: and at about midway we met the SteamBoat from Norwich, bound down to Yarmouth: between which places there is a daily interchange at 3/- for best cabin (forward) & 2/- for the inferior (which is at the aftermast part). We arrived at 1/4 past 2 being about 5 hours, & going by the winding of the River about thirty miles. The small Boat [29] is sent on shore on any passengers desiring admission, or with any one desirous to leave. We received on board One Gentleman who, somehow led to it, perhaps by casual observation, avowed himself a Roman Catholic, and growing warm in the praise of his Community, became equally warm against the Protestants, affirming Luther to have been one of the worst men that ever lived, and that he died actually <u>drunk</u>!! He was not sparing in affirmation that the Protestant Scriptures were false & that Catholic children were better instilled than others, & at last justified fresh atrocities by the oppression of Luther under which Catholics groaned from Protestant power.

Our Company, forward, was but of 8 grown persons, & 3 children, yet, even here, there was a subject of sorrow: a young woman with her Infant only three weeks old was going to Norwich to see the corpse of her Father!

Taking their leave of Yarmouth, Marten and his family board another steamboat, bound this time for Norwich via the river Yare. The passenger service from Yarmouth to Norwich had begun in 1813 with the SS *Experiment*. Competition for trade soon increased, and captains would try to beat the record time. On April 4th 1817 the ship *Telegraph* blew up during such an attempt, causing the loss of thirteen lives.

For centuries parts of the river Yare had been unsuitable for seaborne vessels, and in 1814 a project had been started to open up such communication. A plan was submitted to the Norwich Corporation to make Norwich a port once again by way of Yarmouth. However, in 1818, after the necessary surveys had been completed, it was decided to avoid Yarmouth and open a link between Norwich and Lowestoft. Yarmouth Corporation spent £8,000 opposing this new scheme, but the Norwich and Lowestoft Navigation was opened in 1833.

# 3
# Norwich

## The Georgian city break

On entering the Norfolk Hotel[1] where we purposed remaining we were met by Dr Y. who kindly pressed us to see him, but as our time was limitted, and our object was to be quite free of engagements that we might rove at our fancy, we declined the proffered & hospitable kindness.

We took a turn in the busy Market & by the Castle etc in the Evening. Weather very fine.

The Marten family arrived in Norwich at a time when the city, like the rest of the country, was on the brink of a protracted recession. Between 1800 and 1830 the city's population grew from 37,000 to 61,000. Whereas in the eighteenth century Norwich was a thriving city with a prosperous textile industry, by 1830 riots and machine breaking were rife amongst the city's weavers, and unemployment was the fate of many. Some visitors continued to praise the city's beauty and standing, seemingly oblivious to the plight of her major industry, weaving. J. Callcott Horsley referred to Norwich in 1836 as 'that most interesting and picturesque old city'. In his *Norfolk and Suffolk Journal* (1821) William Cobbett wrote that he was particularly impressed with the cleanliness and quality of the market and with the 'truly majestic Castle'.

[31] Sunday 11th September

We went to Mr Kinghorn's meeting at St. Mary's. It has a handsome porch in front & the inside roof is arched like a Gothic Cathedral. Doubtless meant to look very handsome and grand, but upon such a diminutive scale – and only Lath[2] [?&] plaister of a hungry look & with many a plaister crack – the small pillars supporting the points of the Gothic droop over the galleries fluted and discovering many an open shake in the wood – the whole appeared like a design-abortive – and [thought] that plainness would have been the surer elegance. Mr Kinghorn prayed in a very pleasing manner – his preaching was not to us so satisfactory – it was Essayish rather than experimental or practical & there wanted, as we all thought, a seriousness in [32] his deportment. He appeared to us more the preacher than the Minister or pastor. His pronunciation is very broad and his action rather restless than animated. His subject XVII John 9/12 "I pray for them – I pray not for the World but for them which thou hast given me" etc etc etc. His principal points were that none merely human could consistently appeal to the "Holy Father" & say to Him – "All mine are thine & thine are mine" – as the Lord Jesus who is the Truth did say – That by the prayer of Christ it is demonstrated that he has a speciality of interest in those whom God had given him in distinction from those who are of the World. The need and the benefit of the prayers of Christ, not only for the Apostles who were so [33] singularly exposed to difficulties and dangers, but to & for all who should thereafter believe in Christ through the testimony which the Apostles should bear – And that Christ would be glorified in the obedient conduct of all true believers both in the World which is – in the day of Judgement & in the high praise of Eternity.

The Congregation [was] about 300 and almost all of genteel appearance.

Mr Kinghorn is a tall, thin old Gentleman – very plain in his attire – simple in appearance – of acknowledged talents and has entered the lists in controversy with Robert Hall of Leicester on the subject of open Communion which is advocated by the latter and opposed by the former. Of these opponents such are the high litterary attainments that the Baptist [34] Denomination may well be somewhat proud of them both.

Whilst residing in Norwich the Martens attended three different religious services or meetings, a habit not uncommon to dissenters. First, they attended a meeting at St Mary's Baptist Chapel in Duke Street led by its minister Joseph Kinghorn (1766-1832). Built in 1744, St Mary's soon became the leading Baptist chapel in Norwich, where members were said to enjoy a family relationship and enviable social life. St Mary's also had a well-attended Sunday School and a Mutual Benefit Society to help members in financial difficulties. Such was its popularity that a second, larger, chapel was built in 1812, being enlarged to seat 1000 people in 1823. This chapel was destroyed by bombing in 1942, but rebuilt in 1952.

Dissenting taste in church architecture was generally along the lines of Marten's view that 'plainness would have been the surer elegance', the building being somewhat insignificant compared to the congregation. Many nonconformist meetings began in rooms and warehouses, indeed the congregation of St Mary's first met in a granary in Coslany. The newly rebuilt meetinghouse of 1811 was described as 'altogether both within and without one of the handsomest meeting houses in the kingdom', yet pleasingly free 'from all popery and popish adornments'.[3]

Joseph Kinghorn's ministry, it is said, was 'calculated to make stalwart Bible Christians who knew what they believed and why'.[4] Kinghorn became something of a legendary figure, renowned for his piety and scholarship and held in 'affectionate veneration' by his congregation. Although prayer took up a large part of his services, which were usually about two hours long, preaching was considered of paramount importance. Unfortunately, the Martens found his preaching less than satisfactory, but there were said to be many 'sturdy nonconformists in Norwich . . . who held Mr Kinghorn in high esteem'.[5] One of his congregation, Cecilia Brightwell, observed of Kinghorn's preaching that 'he fixed the attention of his hearers by the peculiar manner in which he treated his subject', concluding that 'what he said left an abiding impression'.

Although Kinghorn read widely on theology and was considered one of the foremost Hebrew scholars of his day, he often tended to be conservative doctrinally. When the Baptist minister Robert Hall (1764–1831) published his *On Terms of Communion* in 1816 stating the case for 'Open' Communion for the unbaptised, Kinghorn replied with *Baptism, a Term of Communion at the Lord's Supper*. The argument eventually went in favour of Hall, who however acknowledged that his opponent's work was the best defence of Closed Communion he had ever read. St Mary's later became embroiled in a lawsuit on this subject, disturbing the members and diverting the attention of its minister George Gould.

**In the Evening, although it rained smartly, we went to Princes Street meeting. This also has a Porch and fluted Pillars (these are of cast Iron), but the ceiling is quite plain & has a sober and consistent appearance. It is larger than Mr**

Kinghorn's. The Revd. Mr Alexander, formerly of Hoxton, preach'd from the 15th of Exodus containing Moses' sublime song of triumphant praise on the deliverance of Israel and the destruction of the Egyptians in the Red Sea. His sermon rivetted the attention because not only of the excellence but of the very instructive nature of his observations.

[35] He discoursed upon the many proofs of the Fact – the nature and tendency of infidelity – the compliance which true faith gives to the Commands of God even when appearances are forbidding. It was when the feet of the obedient were touching the stream that the waters divided. The Israelites did but that which is now continually doing – when new trouble came they forgot past wondrous works & doubted continuing love and power. This he rebuked with much ability and finally brought the Congregation to look forward to that day which should terminate the days of each when the swellings of Jordan should be in the front – difficulties on difficulties appear piled on either hand – a wily, artful, malicious and menacing [36] Enemy be in close pursuit – and yet where no possibility appeared for retreat – and the evident Command of God appear'd that the soul should go forward – that then they should call to mind the power and love of the Angel of the Covenant and remember that once on Canaan's blessed shore – the believer should add to the triumphant song of Moses the more elevated song of salvation by the Lamb – in a chorus which should be without weariness and without termination.

We had a wet and a dark walk home but we felt amply repaid by the instruction & pleasure which we had received.

Before the 1820s the streets of Norwich were so badly lit that there was little inducement for the nonconformists to hold evening meetings. Kinghorn was the first to introduce such meetings to Norwich, these proving so popular that other chapels soon took up the idea as street lighting was improved in this decade with the introduction of gas.

Marten appears to have been rather more impressed with the preaching of John Alexander (1797–1868) on his visit to the Independent Prince's Street Chapel. Alexander was a firm believer in the principle that 'churches exist not only for preserving and professing the truths of the Gospel but for propagating them'; consequently, his ministry in Norwich was described as being 'vigorously evangelical'.[6] Known for having an overflowing audience on the Sunday and an 'active vitality' all the week, Alexander was also seen as Norwich's second bishop, being perfectly at home in company with the city's great and good.

The foundation stone of the Prince's Street Chapel had been laid in 1819, but within a few years the cheap construction was starting to show, and more money had to be spent in strengthening the roof. Such was the popularity of its young preacher that in 30 years the congregation increased from 14 to 300. In addition to supporting two other chapels, a Sunday School, a Society for the Sick and Poor, and a Christian Instruction Society, the chapel raised £22,500 for works of Christian charity during these years. A tea party was held in St Andrew's Hall, attended by 800 people, to celebrate the 30-year ministry of 'a faithful and zealous pastor'.[7]

## [37] Monday 12 September

**At quarter past 10 o'clock we attended the Cathedral service which was the same as in other Cathedrals. There were scarcely a dozen persons beside the ecclesiastics who officiated. The Building is in fair preservation considering that it has been [here] since the year 1096. The interior is very clean and from the magnitude and architecture presents to the Eye a solemn grandeur – The Courts & inclosures and ancient Houses round it are also kept in that order & have that still and quiet aspect & that appearance of retirement and comfort which is [38] usually found around County Cathedrals.**

In stark contrast to the activities of the nonconformist congregations of early nineteenth-century Norwich was the state of neglect to be found at the Cathedral. Although Marten notices with pleasure the order and stillness surrounding the building, he also notes that, in common with many other cathedrals, the congregation was pitifully small. Criticism of the Cathedral was running high in this period; in some circles Norwich became known mockingly as the 'Dead See'! The Cathedral was rebuked for being 'drearily respectable', and for not fulfilling its role as a Christian centre. A later visitor commented that 'Nothing can be worse than the irreverent, careless and undevotional character of worship in the parish church of the diocese', summing up, 'A more cold and miserable service I have seldom heard'.[8]

**We then walk'd about the large City & came by St. Giles' Church into Heigham and called on Mr. Grout who permitted us to go through his important Silk Manufactury. The works are in several floors and the winding, twisting, bobbinning etc. are by Machinery moved by a beautiful 20 Horse Power Engine.[9.] These operations are watched and conducted by**

more than seventy females, some so young as 7 to 8 years of age. These are on [39] foot from seven in the Morning till Eight in the Evening watching the threads, repairing the broken [threads] & seeing that all go[es] on well – occasionally supplying Oil when wanted to prevent evil from friction – Only that they have ½ an hour to breakfast & an hour for Dinner – And these little Girls earn some 5/-, some 5/6 per week. We then were shewn the winding into warp, the subsequent Beaming, & the reeds for the Weaving, and were informed that a Yard wide Crape has in that breadth 2560 single twisted threads of silk. We then saw one of the female superintendants at her Crape loom and afterwards [40] the turners shop where nine men were employed in preparing Bobbins etc etc etc for the Factory here & the much larger which Mr. Grout is now erecting at Yarmouth.[10] The silk used here is principally from Bengal but part was the white silk from China.

Seeing a loom going in a private House as we passed we asked the woman, who was weaving Norwich crape & learned that she could, by close application weave Eleven yards each day, but we omitted to ask her earning by that work.

Marten's description of his visit to the silk factory of Grout and Company of Lower Westwick Street and New Mills Yard is interesting for it mentions people as well as processes. The subject would probably have intrigued the diarist who started his working life in the counting house of an Italian silk merchant. Grout's was described as a 'silk firm of the largest size in England', employing 800 people in spinning, 200 in weaving, plus many others.[11] As the diarist records, although wages were reasonably good, hours were long, and conditions often unfavourable, with the employment of young children being a common practice.

The 1820s were uncertain times for those working in the Norwich textile industry. Competition from Yorkshire and Lancashire weavers was gradually eroding the city's monopoly in the manufacture of worsted cloth, whilst the effects of the Napoleonic Wars seriously disrupted markets for the following 20 years. Norwich suddenly found itself unable to compete with the technological innovations and factory organisation of its rivals, yet, ironically, the introduction of power looms put hundreds of its weavers out of work. By the 1830s many handloom weavers were impoverished and forced to apply for Poor Relief.

It has been estimated that in the period 1815-45 there were 3,600 looms still in use in private houses in Norwich.[12] Weavers who worked at home, like the woman observed by the Martens, worked between 12 and 14 hours a day, the hours varying with the amount of daylight available. In the 1820s, Norwich manufacturers were forced to diversify, turning away from the traditional worsted cloth in favour of higher quality, handmade, fashionable crepes and black silks. The latter, made specifically as mourning fabrics, helped to sustain the fortunes of the city's struggling handloom weavers throughout the nineteenth century.

**[41] We strolled thence to the confines of the Town Northward till we came to the Fields & found the population lively – the small sharp stones with which the streets are paved very annoying – and churches so abounding that the Eye could scarcely fail to see two or three whichever way it turned. Many of these are flint faced and some of them with squared flints very carefully cut & nicely laid. We counted Eleven steeples from our chamber window.**

An 1842 guidebook to Norwich states that one of the peculiarities of the city is the irregularity and narrowness of its streets. The author comments that 'there is scarcely any place of importance in England in which the streets are in a worse condition than those in Norwich'. An Improvement Commission had been set up in 1806 to make improvements to the paving, lighting and cleaning of the streets, but the work was beset with interruptions. In 1825 a new Improvement Act allowed higher rates to be levied on property for these purposes.

**In the Evening we wandered through the Eastward & Southward parts of the City and saw many very large and elegant Houses. Being asked [42] by two Italian Image Lads to buy an Image of Walter Scott – a Bust of natural size which was offered for a shilling – I conversed with them in their own tongue which appeared to gratify them. I learned that they were natives of Florence – had walked in five days from London – had brought their Goods on their heads & had sold all but a Walter Scott, a Shakespeare, a Milton, & a Lord Byron. As I could not buy, I presented them with a few pence, for which they expressed their thanks very pleasingly.**

[43] Tuesday 13 September

**We purposed obtaining permission to mount the top of the elevated Castle in order to have a panoramic view of the City & the Hills which surround it, but we were dissuaded on account of the wind blowing so strong that it would be difficult to stand against it. We therefore walk'd round the Castle on the Mount which is lofty enough to afford a view over the Houses and to the**

distant Hills. Here we counted 23 steeples of the 36 churches which the Map of Norwich states to be in it, and prolonged our stay because of the pleasure we enjoyed. There was however some alloy in seeing the Bars and fastnesses[13] preparing for the securing [44][of] future <u>County</u> Offenders – the Castle, the Mount & the fosse round it belonging, not to the City but to the County.

Norwich had long had a reputation for unrest and revolution, bribery and corruption being common during elections, with radicalism easily stirred by events in France. Violent crime was on the increase in the 1820s, and machine-breaking, rioting and attacks on strike-breakers boosted admissions to the county gaol by 30% in 1831-32. Norwich's Norman castle had been used to house prisoners long before 1824 when plans were drawn up for using it as the county gaol. The diarist was not the only observer to voice objections to this plan. Amongst others, the United Friars Society unanimously opposed these changes at one of their 1821 meetings. However, once completed in 1828, the prison, designed by William Wilkins, was described as being 'commodious, and well-adapted for the health and regulation of the prisoners'.[14]

**We had afterwards a pleasant walk by Surr[e]y Street & past the Norfolk and Norwich Hospital & partly on the Road towards London where it divides, one Branch leading through Ipswich and the other through Newmarket.**

**We noticed in many places remnants of the ancient walls of the City, partly built upon, & in places used to train fruit-trees.**

William Fellowes has long been regarded as the founder the Norfolk and Norwich Hospital in 1771 for the relief of the sick and the lame poor of both city and county. The architect was Thomas Ivory, who gave his services free of charge. At first there were 120 beds, but for several years only two-thirds of these appear to have been in use. The philanthropist and prison reformer John Howard wrote of his visit in 1789, 'This spacious infirmary was perfectly neat and clean; the beds not crowded; the wards quiet and fresh; and the dietary hung up. A notable matron; there are about ninety beds; at my last visit fifty-two were occupied.'

Sturdy flint walls, portions of which can still be seen today, formerly protected Norwich. At one time the wall had 40 towers, 12 gates and a wide ditch running round the outside. In 1792 the city gates and parts of the wall were pulled down, partly in order to help air to circulate in the city, a precaution justified by the belief that many diseases were caused by stale and unpleasant odours.

The City is now building a new Gaol near St. Giles' & a wing of it is expected to be inhabited towards [45] the close of this Year. We were admitted to go over the whole Building. The Governor's House is in the Center, and from the several windows he can at all times inspect every part of the Prison. The Chapel is in the Governor's House. His pew is opposite & very close to the Pulpit which is entered from the winding staircase. The Felons are in Pews, even with the Governor, whose Eye may be constantly on them, and the Twinkeys [?Turnkeys] guard the two entrances during the whole of the divine service. The Debtors are on the floor of the Chapel, and thus every one can see & hear the Preacher. We were shown the cells for the Felons who are confined at night separately – but they have a Day-Room & they have the privilege of the open air in a Yard [46] allotted to them. Condemned Felons left for execution have other & still stronger lonesome cells which they are not permitted to leave until the hour when they are taken to the platform over the entrance Gate to surrender their forfeited lives to the violated justice of their Country. As there may be Debtors of a superior class there are small rooms which may be hired for four shillings per week & in which when they please they may remain alone and without interruption from other Debtors. We saw a room preparing as a Bath in which every prisoner on entrance is washed thoroughly, his clothes taken away from him, & he is then habited in the Gaol-dress and is kept sometime before he is permitted to [47] associate with his fellow Prisoners. A large tank is to be filled by the Force-Pump by the labor of the Prisoners and from this, water will be conveyed through the whole Building. We imagined this to be on the plan of the Penitentiary near Chelsea.[15] There is a spacious Infirmary for the sick & the whole of this great expense is at the cost, being for the use of, the City.

The Marten family were obviously impressed with the utilitarian design of the 'New Gaol and House of Correction' on Earlham Road, constructed between 1824 and 1827. The prison was designed by local architect Philip Barnes and was probably based on the model Millbank Penitentiary based on the ideas of reformer Jeremy Bentham. Comprising 114 cells, and enclosing an acre of ground, the prison cost between £23,000 and £30,000. With its dayroom, baths, chapel and exercise yard, the prison obviously put some emphasis on health, cleanliness, and godliness. In 1878 the Prison Commissioners decided to remove the prisoners to the county gaol and sell the building and the land at public auction. Today the Roman Catholic Cathedral, St John's, occupies the site.

The principal streets in Norwich are with flat pavements for the foot passengers – but the greatest number are paved with small pebbles and flints uneasy to the foot and on which one unused cannot walk either steadily or comfortably. We were not accosted in any of our walks even by a single mendicant. Every body seemed busy [48] and we were told by a Gentleman, a resident, that no complaints were heard and that the Manufactures and general business of the place were in thriving condition. Houses of the third and forth rate & some even beneath these were building to a great extension of Norwich, a circumstance which marks many other Cities beside this.

Despite the troubles in the textile industry, and thanks to periodic recoveries in the economy, between 1819 and 1826 Norwich was said to be in the midst of a 'building boom'. In the 1820s, speculators began to build larger and more ordered estates in the city, concentrating mainly on providing smaller houses for working people. During a walk around the city the diarist observes the building activity taking place in the north-west side of Newmarket Road which was gradually filling up with houses in the period 1820–40.

Our stay at Norwich has been pleasant – and the Norfolk Hotel is entitled to praise for the goodness of its provisions, the neatness of its accommodation, and the attention of its Conductors & Servants. We were also perfectly satisfied with the reasonableness of its charges.

# 4
# Cromer

## Locals, lighthouses and lobsters

[49] We left the Hotel at 20 minutes before 4 o'clock in the stage for Cromer. Our companion (for the stage held but four inside) was a woman of about 60 who had had a paralytic stroke and was going to Thorpe[1] in hope of gaining strength and health. She was accompanied to the coach by her son whose kind look spoke filial affection but much mingled with apparent & sorrowful apprehension. It rained when we started & continued for some time. Our road was pleasant as the foliage & herbage & turnips had by the recent rains recovered from the effects of the unusual summer heats.[2] We went around through North Walsham making about 26 miles to Cromer where we arrived at nearly 8 o'clock enjoying for a mile or two the sight of the light from Cromer Light House.

[50] We put up at the New Inn where the coach stopped & found it a most comfortable place. It was built by the landlord - makes up above 40 beds - is well furnished - has some pretty little sitting rooms - every appearance of ample means and a good spirit for the accommodation of guests who are waited upon by the Landlord's handsome, neat & well behaved daughters - & has greatly surpassed our expectations of Cromer's comforts. The Landlord [said] that when he came (from Truro) there were here but 9 lodging Houses & that there are now 70 - that duty was done in the church once in a [51] fortnight, sometimes only (once) in three weeks, once five weeks lapsed

between the services, but now, Sir, said he, we have a Gospel Preacher & duty regularly every Sabbath morning and afternoon & the church well attended, and I have been church warden more than twelve years. It is good men, Sir, whom we want in our churches who will not only do their duty well in their pulpits, but who will walk well and circumspectly when out of them.

### Wednesday 14th September

A thick mist over the sea impenitrable by the Eye at a half-mile's distance. A Boat came in this morning with Herrings, the catch [52] of the past night. There are seven Bathing Machines, warm & cold Baths and shower Baths, a subscription Room on the Beach, a Life Boat on wheels ready for an instant start to the water, a Pier of about 200 feet long, well floored for a promenade, and altho' the sea may be said to be little more than undulating, the waves roll in with a noble break and the pebbles speak loudly as the water forced on shore returns to meet the succeeding swell.

Taking their leave of Norwich for a week or so, the Marten family travel by coach to Cromer. Approaching the town they are impressed, as many visitors have been, by the bright light issuing from the town's first lighthouse. Edward Bowel of Ipswich first lit this coal fired lighthouse in 1719, replacing a fire beacon positioned on the church tower as a guide to shipping. The lighthouse that adorns Cromer's cliffs today was built in 1833 when the earlier building was threatened by the encroaching sea, finally succumbing in 1866.

First, and subsequent, impressions of Cromer's New Inn appear to have been favourable. This was one of the town's first sizeable hotels, and had been run as such certainly before the 1780s, being known at various times as the 'Royal Oak' and 'Tucker's Hotel'. The landlord referred to here was George Cooke Tucker, who had recently taken over and rebuilt the hotel.

It is interesting to note the diarist's comment that his expectations of 'Cromer's comforts' were greatly exceeded. Edmund Bartell's *Cromer Considered as a Watering Place* (1806) reported that 'the want of a large and well conducted inn' was preventing the town from rivalling the popularity of other bathing places. By the time of Catherine Ward's 1823 novel, *The Cottage on the Cliff*, though, Cromer had become 'the resort of the most fashionable company at the bathing seasons'. William White observed in his *Norfolk Directory* of 1845 that Cromer had improved considerably, stating that it now 'ranks as one of the most fashionable sea-bathing places in the kingdom'.

*Cromer from the end of the pier. Tucker's hotel, where Mr Marten was staying, is the building obscuring the body of the church. The building at the top of the zig-zag path up the cliff on the right is Lord Suffield's marine villa, which in 1830 was to become the Hotel de Paris. All the pictures in this chapter are Marten's own sketches included in his Journal.*

Cromer was, and is, no stranger to fierce autumnal gales, those of 1789 and 1823 in particular resulting in the wrecking of many ships. Efforts to reduce such recurrent tragedies had begun in 1804 when Lord Suffield raised subscriptions to launch the county's first lifeboat. During a gale of 1810, the lifeboat and crew rescued 14 men and one woman from the Brig *Anna*. By 1823, the lifeboat had performed her third rescue, and additional boats had been established at Winterton and Yarmouth.

A Bath House had recently been built on the beach by Thomas Randell, providing visitors with hot and cold seawater baths and showers. The subscription reading room had been built in 1814. A terrible storm of February 1836 washed the building away, killing an unfortunate man trying to rescue the furniture. The town's first bathing machine was owned by Terry & Pearson and had appeared on the beach in 1779. By the 1830s there were ten machines. The new jetty or pier, begun in 1822 and estimated to have cost £1,400, had been much praised as exhibiting 'a magnificent proof of the skill of the engineer', ironfounder William Haze of Saxthorpe, but it too was eventually destroyed by the sea.

The Church has a noble square Tower, very lofty and in good repair. The West End of the Body of the church is in desolate ruin but the part which [53] did formerly council with it is now built up – thus shortning the length of the interior by all that which is now cut off. There is a Boarding Hotel[3] and some very good private Houses – a terrace toward the sea with new & convenient Houses, some of which are let, & others yet to be hired. The White Flag, as is sometimes termed at watering places, the "Lodgings to let" does not appear much at the windows, and in my cruize of discovery this morning I was not very successful in gaining, as I was ordered, intelligence on this subject for the Ladies subsequent determination.

It appears from the account of Cromer[4] that the Town of Shipdon which was superior to Cromer with its Parish Church dedicated to St. Peter has been destroyed by the encroachments of the sea and that [54] at very low tides the Rock called by the Fishermen the Church Rock shews some remnants of a Building and is supposed to be the site of that Parish Church. The destruction is said to have taken place about the reign of Henry IV. The cliffs are now frequently falling into the sea, and such are the changes that where there are now deep Bays there were once bold & lofty projecting headlands.

The present church is dedicated to the two great Apostles, St. Peter & St. Paul, and was erected in the 16th year of the second Richard. Its Tower is 150 feet high. The church was 200 feet long and its inside as rich in ornament as the outside is beautiful by the excellence [55] of the flintwork. In Cromwell's time the church was used as a Barrack and then sadly defaced.

Cromer once belonged to the much larger parish of Shipden, which, as the diarist says, was engulfed by the sea during the reign of Henry IV (1399–1413). The town had already begun to develop during the fourteenth century, by which time building of the present church was under way. The dedication to St Peter and St Paul was in memory of St Paul's of Shipden juxta Felbrigge which stood on the present Cromer site, and St Peter's of Shipden juxta Mare.

An example of early Perpendicular architecture, the church is one of the largest in the county. After the Reformation the building had fallen into decline, the chancel was demolished and building materials sold off. By 1767 much of the roof over the nave and aisles had collapsed. At the end of the eighteenth century the tide of neglect was turning with the building of the west gallery and a new organ. The church was completely restored under Rev. Frederic Fitch (1852–96).

The Cliffs near Cromer are in many parts lofty and well broken; and as the Courses of the Trades from Newcastle, Sunderland, Scotland, the Baltic, etc are well in to the Shore, it is rare, on a clear day, to find a scarcity in the view of shipping at sea. The fog has, however, been so much of the Newfoundland-Bank-kind, that if there were ships they were invisible to us.

The Light House is distant about a Mile: built of Brick: three stories high: has 15 Lamps, each in a reflector 18 Inches in diameter: are moved by clockwork, by which 5 Lamps give a full blaze every minute, & by which it is distinguished [56] from the other numerous lights on this coast. We took some pains to day to procure comfortable lodgings, but did not find any to tempt us away from the Inn, whose excellent accommodation & ready attentions we have experienced; and we, therefore, have determined, while at Cromer, to continue at the "New Inn".


Thursday 15th September

The scenery this morning was the more pleasant from the contrast which it formed with the cloudy mist of yesterday. On rising we beheld a full & gently swelling sea, with a clear line of Horizon, and ships, near & distant, smoothly [57] advancing to their several destinations. The sunshine was bright and warm; and after a turn or two on the Pier, and taking a slight sketch from its end, seaward, we walk'd on the cliff-tops to lower Runton, & then nearly to upper Runton, and back to the Town. There were, at one time, more than thirty of the Boats from Cromer fishing in the offing, but through the day there were few ships passing. We were pleased with the Country as we viewed it round, and at one place near the cliff a covey of ten Partridges rose suddenly with the usual noise of their taking wing. They were disturbed by our close approach, & fled not knowing that we were not [58] of those who sought their destruction.

As the Church at Cromer & the Light House beyond it offered a noticeable view as we sat on a bank on the cliff to rest ourselves, we took a slight sketch of these with the Jetty, or pier, of Cromer then just in sight: & then we descended by a Gate, or opening, in the cliff to the sands, along which we returned to Cromer often stopping to view the lofty cliff, or the large masses of land which had fallen through the underminings of the wash of the sea. The children of the neighbourhood offered to our purchase small pebbles

*Cromer from the west, as seen by the Martens from the hill between 'Lower' (East) Runton and 'Upper' (West) Runton. The lighthouse is on the horizon, the top of Cromer church tower clearly visible and the jetty projecting from behind the cliff. Closer to the artist, the houses in the dip on the right are those of East Runton. Much of the cliff has fallen victim to coastal erosion since Marten's day.*

**which they had selected from the shore & which they dignified with the appellation of Cornelians [Carnelians]; a Countryman offered as a curiosity-stone a piece of common granite which [59] he wished us to purchase.**[5]

Walking and sketching appear to have taken up a lot of the Martens' time whilst in Cromer. Indeed, this was true of the typical Georgian tourist, who was always on the lookout for the 'picturesque' view to capture on paper, just as the modern holidaymaker captures memories on camera. Marten's sketches show an eye for detail, and his accuracy suggests that he might have used an optical drawing aid, the camera lucida, invented in 1807.

Here again the true Georgian explorer, Marten appears to have been somewhat bemused by the local people he encounters. He is particularly entertained by the efforts of some opportunist locals to sell him pieces of stone from the beach. Similarly, a character in Catherine Ward's 1823 novel comments wryly, when referring to visiting gentry spending their money in the town, 'the inhabitants of Cromer are likely to have a fine harvest'.

On our return we perceived the approach of a returning North-East mist & which soon enveloped us, to the exclusion of our sea prospects.

The more we look at the edifice of the Church the more we are pleased with the taste and skill of the Architect: but it really grieves us to see the sculptured stones now used as wall-coping, & in many instances as fending-stones at the Doors of private Houses.

We dined today on hot Lobsters used by us for the first time as fish for a first course: a good thing is a good thing at all times, & hot lobsters, or cold lobsters, are good things; and if a real relish, & making good use of hot lobsters, fresh, of course, and in fine condition, can entitle them to praise, ours of today fearlessly claim the title of excellent food. [60] Read today from a London newspaper of the marriage at Smyrna on the 22nd July of my young Friend John Warmington to Miss Grace Louisa, eldest daughter of John Barker Esq.re, His Britannic Majesty's Consul for Aleppo and its dependencies – may it prove as I trust it will a very happy union.

I walked on the Pier this Evening at High Water and found the full light of the Light House which occurred every minute cheering and pleasant.

Near to the Pier there is, far within High Water Mark, a strong tank in which Lobsters are preserved alive 'till wanted for use. The [61] Boats which go off this Town catch Cod, Soals, Turbots, & Lobsters. The latter are sold by the pound weight & usually about 8d per lb. We have had but little Fish for sale since our arrival.

There is no appearance of Rock here but the cliffs are all of soft Earth of various kinds – some of a very sapponaceous[6] appearance & every where evidence of frequent & extensive falls to the beach.


Friday 16th September 1825

The earlier part of this morning misty and unpromising – we all had a walk on the Jetty early and not without company. I sketch'd the easternmost part of the Coast & while my Ladies were preparing for walking did the same from

*Above:*
The easternmost part of Cromer, viewed from the end of the jetty. Buildings shown include (left to right): the lighthouse; the coastguards' station with its flagpole; Beach House in its original two-storey form at the foot of the Gangway (it was later to be extended to three storeys and called Marine View); the Crescent on the clifftop; and Thomas Randell's seawater bath house on stilts on the beach.

*Below:*
Cromer's west cliffs, from the end of the pier.

[62] the Pier of the western cliffs. Saw the boats launching to visit the Lobster Pots which had been left during the night at sea. A Fisherman returned from the visit with a tolerably sized hand Basket full of lively Lobsters. These Potts are baited (as I learned from a fisherman's Boy) with Butts. On enquiring what Butts were he told me they were like sandlings. As this brought me no nearer to the knowledge I desired I was obliged to renew my enquiry. The good natured Boy seemed to wonder somewhat at my ignorance & told me they were small fish, flat like a flounder or a small turbot, and that these were very good for catching Lobsters. He was about to immerse in the sea a Basket containing live Lobsters, the Basket being first made fast to the [63] Jetty. He said that the live Lobsters would bite very hard unless they took the precaution which they generally used on first catching them of tying down their claws. He had had his finger lately bitten – and the Lobsters would, unless prevented, bite one another when they were confined.

We visited a fish curing House and examined the Liverpool salt which was in store: saw them preparing the cod for salting: and had a peep into the smoaky place where, by the smoak, <u>blue</u> Herrings were converted into <u>red</u> Herrings. The place was such a dense cloud that the Herrings then under operation were wholly invisible.

The sky cleared to a pleasant day. The wind had changed to the southward & westward & many ships soon appeared coming round from by Yarmouth roads making for the north. We had at one time 26 Vessels in view under sail & more than 40 fishing Boats on the sea & some with parties.

[64] Our purposed walk to the Light House led us past the Preventive Service Station House near which we noticed some of the narrow and Eggshell like Boats for fast rowing with which this service is supplied. We could not but admire while looking at them what apparently slender defence there is for these men when obliged to go on perhaps a rough sea in pursuit in vessels of such slight strength – so narrow & so liable to accident.

Robert Marten was by no means the only visitor to have commented on the excellence of Cromer's lobsters. In 1720 Daniel Defoe wrote that he knew of little else for which the town was famous! Cromer had long been a fishing village and small port before its rise as a seaside resort. For many years crabs and lobsters were the basis of its fishing industry, but over-fishing eventually led to the enforcement of a closed season. Herrings remained an important catch, and in 1845 there were still four fish curing houses like the one visited by the diarist.

Enjoying a stroll along the beach, Marten notices the boats of the town's customs & excise, or coastguard, officers. Smuggling, particularly of liquor, had been on the increase since the late eighteenth century, and its detection or 'prevention' could sometimes prove perilous for the customs officers involved. Despite large seizures of goods, the determined smugglers continued to be well organised and highly successful off Cromer, even being prepared to manhandle the heavy Dolphin post that marked the manor boundaries out of the way. On one Friday in 1779 over 50 men landed thirteen cargoes of contraband, including spirits and tea, valued at several thousand pounds.

**In a field belonging we believe to Mr. Hoare[7] & on which we were perhaps trespassers we found a commodious seat on an eminence & commanding a delightful view seaward & towards the Town. It would not do to be idle with such advantages, & to improve time a sketch was made of the scenery towards the Town. That toward the sea was very inviting but the sameness of [65] a sea prospect on a calm day prevented even a wish to copy it.**

**Two Huntsmen were giving their ten couple of hounds the benefit of the sea air by treating them with a run on the sands.**

**With some toil we reach'd at length the Cromer Light House which <u>Mrs Newstead</u> informed us was 270 feet above the level of the sea, as we supposed**

*Cromer viewed from the land belonging to Mr Hoare.*

High Water, but we did not enquire as to the fact. She had lived there more than thirty years. The Family consists of four, & one sits up alternately during the hours when the Lights should be kept burning. We saw the nature of the clock work which keeps the Lamps-frame continually & equally turning so as to give the full light of five large reflected Lamps every minute.

[66] To please Old Lady Newstead who presented us with some seeds of the Wax-Work Piony [Peony] in return for some tracts presented to her I took a sketch of the Light House & promised to make a copy for her. The <u>five</u> Lights make but <u>one</u> at a distance and that so powerful, & being so elevated as to be seen &

*Mrs & Miss Marten walking to the lighthouse.*

known by a ship when thirty miles from the Land. The apartments are small & shaped to the form of the House but they were quite worthy of notice for their cleanliness & good order as well as for the quality of the furniture.

Our return led us near to the pretty residences of the Gurneys – the Buxtons – the Barclays & Hoares who annually spend some months in this place.[8]

[67] Towards the Evening a large fleet of vessels were passing us bound to the northward, so that there appeared almost a continual line of Brigs, (most probably light Colliers) from the point of vision in the East to the full reach of the Eye westward, which, with the return of the fishing Boats, and the busy scene of landing the nets, and the several catches of fish; the carrying [of] the Boats themselves by hand to a place of safety for the night, and the fast rising tide breaking its constantly succeeding waves upon the pebbly

*View from a window of the New Inn, Cromer.*

**beach, rendered our Evening watch on the Jetty amusing & pleasant. At the moment of writing this – the nearly High-Water is roaring & foaming almost beneath our window, not displeasing to the Ear, nor interrupting to the thoughts which employ the Pens of the Ladies in their epistolary labors.**

Although a rather winding route, it is probable that the Marten family walked back to Cromer via Northrepps. This walk was in fact recommended by Edmund Bartell in his 1806 guide and became an established favourite with visitors. Bartell claims that the view on returning from this walk is one of the most advantageous, stating, 'The composition is good, the prospect rich, and the whole finely set off by a grand Marine distance.'

Many observers of Cromer testified to the almost constant presence of shipping off the coast. The 1867 guide states 'The sea at Cromer is almost always diversified by a change of moving objects; the trade from Newcastle, Sunderland and the Baltic keeping up a constant succession of vessels; to which may be added the regular appearance of the various steam-vessels which ply between London and the Northern parts'. Watching the fishermen land their catch provided a welcome distraction for the Cromer visitor, breaking up the usual round of walks on the pier, beach, and cliffs. A much later visitor, Clement Scott, noted the continuation of this routine: 'it was the rule to go on the sands in the morning, to walk on one cliff for a mile in the afternoon, to take another mile in the other direction at sunset and to crowd upon the little pier at night.'[9]

[68] Cromer and its neighbourhood is built principally of Boulder-stones, some flint & a little Brick. The Houses, walls, sties[?] are mostly of Boulder stone in coarse mortar which is here and there stuck pretty full of slivers of Flint. In some old buildings the Flint has been squared & the joints as neat as in the very best Brickwork.

### Saturday 17th September

A fine morning, inducing to a walk on the Jetty before breakfast. There were several Ladies walking, and if not in full dress yet, in dresses evincing care, and custom to appear well dressed.

While at Breakfast one window commanded a wide view [69] of the Ocean. Many vessels were making the most they could of a southwest gentle Breeze carrying some to the northward & others south. The Steam Boat from Scarborough passed us well in shore & another shewed smoke at 10 or 12 miles distance from us.

Being pleased with the retired situation of the residence of Joseph Gurney Esq. M.P. for Norwich my Ladies requested a sketch for a memorial & with which I complied.

*The Grove, Joseph Gurney's Cromer residence.*

When John Gurney brought his family to Cromer on holiday in 1793 he began a pattern of long-standing influence and patronage. Joseph Gurney (1755–1830) followed his brother's example and purchased a house on Overstrand Road called 'The Grove'. Whereas in later life Joseph Gurney was known as a strict Quaker, as a young man he was a keen sportsman. He took particular pleasure, it seems, in trying to gauge the number of leaps necessary to descend the steep cliffs at Cromer with his children in tow!

It is quite possible that the Martens were already familiar with the Gurneys and other large nonconformist families who annually visited Cromer, as several lived and worshipped in the Plaistow area. The Buxtons attended the Friends or Quaker meeting at Plaistow where prison reformer Elizabeth Fry (née Gurney) was a regular speaker. Like the Martens, the Friends were great supporters of local schools and charities. Samuel Gurney (1786–1856), who lived nearby at West Ham, was a well known local philanthropist who set aside land around his park for allotments.

*Cromer lighthouse and Miss Marten*

**They (the Ladies) presented Mrs Newstead with the sketch of the Light House with which she appeared much pleased – called her sister directly, [70] said she had very long wished for such a representation, declared it should be framed & glazed, and in her honest thankfulness ask'd if there was any thing to be paid for it, as she would pay for it most willingly. How easy it is sometimes by a little costless attention to confer a favor & give real pleasure. Then ought we not all to look out for, & willingly embrace opportunities where they offer?**

**We walk'd on over a high Headland with an intention**

*Cromer from the Lighthouse Hills: the view seen by the Martens as they returned from Overstrand.*

of getting down to the sands & to return by them to Cromer: but [71] after enjoying the now more extended view Eastward, many vessels coming up from the southward, we met with some large Works under the direction, as we understood, of Lord Suffield,[10] in cutting down the high Cliff to the Beach to make a Carriage way from the sands up to the inland. It appeared to us to be about half done & we have heard that it is now abandoned.

We therefore turned inland and came to the very ancient church of the Parish of Overstrand. The far greater part of this once large Church is in ruins – open to the weather, & walls only left standing [72] of the Easternmost part – a small part next to the Tower at the West End is built up, and roofed, as we suppose, for the use of the Parishioners. These can be but few as the notice affixed to the Church door by order of an Act of the last sessions, gives the names of only three Parishioners (farmers) qualified to serve as Jurors. The once sculptured stones are now used as coping stones, and for head & foot stones for the graves of the Poor. There are in the Tower, & desolate walls, some specimens of very neat squared flint work.

St Martin's was Overstrand's second church, the original being claimed by the sea in the late fourteenth century. By 1845 St Martin's was virtually a ruin, and in 1867 Christchurch was built nearby. The parishioners of Overstrand were, as the diarist correctly observes, few in number, being only 253 by the 1860s. By the end of the nineteenth century, though, Christchurch was becoming inadequate for the large summer congregations, and St Martin's was subsequently rebuilt, opening for worship once again in 1914.

[73] **We had some heavy rain this Evening accompanied with such a lurid glare from the setting sun reflected from the dark clouds, and this again reflected <u>from the sea</u>, as gave the whole atmosphere an appearance almost awful – but it was not accompanied with any Gusts of wind.**

**In my Evening walk on the Jetty a Gentleman acquainted with Cromer joined conversation and remarked that Cromer had one pleasant advantage over most sea side Bathing places – as here the rising of the Sun may be seen from the sea & its setting as <u>in to the sea</u>, & its daily course thus wholly traced.**

[74] **He further noticed that alarm was entertained by many who were less acquainted with the power of the sea as to future probable encroachments on the cliffs nearest to & on which the Houses stand. He said that a House which he pointed out & which has now but a narrow footpath between it & the cliff-edge had only 50 Years since a Carriage Way & a bowling green in the front. And that the new built and still unfinished Jetty (unfinish'd through lack of money) throws the sea so strongly to its eastern side that even an ordinary neap tide tho' with an offshore wind comes up to the cliff foot – and what the [75] future strength of a spring tide or of a series of such tides impelled by a Gale or Gales northerly may be they appear almost to dread conjecture.**

Indulging in topical conversation with one's fellow travellers, or even with the local people, was an integral part of the Georgian holiday. The pier was the place to meet and converse, particularly in the evenings. As the 1867 guide to Cromer states, 'The jetty is the fashionable resort of the evening, the company assembling here; some to enjoy the pure sea breezes, to watch the noble billows as they dash in graceful fury on the beach, the fine spectacle of the setting sun, or the mild splendour of the moon; others to meet their acquaintances, and a few, perhaps . . . for the exercise of their satirical talents.' At this time Cromer was trying hard to foster a select and exclusive rather than a popular image, and even provided visitors lists to enable people to look up suitable companions for their stay.

The diarist shows a considerable interest in the problem of coastal erosion at Cromer. Particularly large cliff falls had taken place in the winter of 1799 and January of 1825, as Marten later discovers. The fears of the resident with whom the diarist converses are well founded, for both the Bath House and the new pier were later washed away by severe storms and high seas, culminating in a successful application for the building of a sea-wall in 1845.

## Sunday the 18th September 1825

The morning is beautiful & so very inviting that while breakfast was preparing I took a little turn. On my return I looked in at the Church seeing the Doors open. The interior is lofty like a Cathedral with aisles & a wide nave – the side Pillars carrying noble Gothic arches. The whole clean, & except where damp had begun a greenish hue, fairly whitewashed. There is a large Organ and a Gallery in the front. The communion table at the East End. The Body of the Church pewed so that unless the [76] worshippers stand up they are not seen by others. I was surprised to find some Ladies so early in the Pews but soon discovered that they had classes of the children of a Sunday School & on enquiry I found that even in this small Town they had about 70 children on the school Books.[11]

In the churchyard is a Tomb of a Mr Larkins of London who had dined at the Inn where we now are in apparant good health – & aged but 43 – retired to his lodgings to rest & was found by his wife at her side in the morning dead & already cold. What a memento for Travellers! The stone bore witness of his excellent character.

I fell interested for the safety of a child of as I supposed about four years of age lying on his face & far more [77] than his head hanging over the edge of the lofty & steep cliff & kicking carelessly & playfully his heels up; & I spoke to a woman, near, to express my apprehensions, and to point out the danger:- but she smiled & said that all the children would do so & that he would come to no harm.

When the Church Bell gave notice of the time to enter it was a pleasing sight to observe the people coming from all parts – all cleanly apparelled but with the gentry and visitors their soon appeared a genteel congregation of perhaps better then 200 persons. The open seats down the centre were well filled with the country folk, & all respectfully & suitably dressed.

The Organ gave, first, a solemn air which challenged the serious attention of the Congregation & at its [78] close Archdeacon Glover commenced the service & after the usual ritual delivered a Gospel sermon in the same

impressive manner in which he read the prayer. His text was from VI
Gal. XV XVI. "For in Christ Jesus neither circumcision availeth anything
nor uncircumcision but a new creature and as many as walk according to
this rule, peace be on them and mercy and upon the Israel of God". He
preached (reading) for about 35 minutes and great stillness pervaded the
whole church. The main drift of the discourse was that if a rite so peculiarly
ordained of God for his peculiar people availed nothing to the Jews – and the
want of it could not prejudice the converted Gentiles [79] – so no present
ordained rites, however in themselves ordained wisely to further greater ends
– No mere attendance upon religious appointments however punctual &
persevered in – in short, no self-righteousness could now avail – but only the
being a new creature. He described the authorized translation as falling far
short of the original. It imported a new building on a new foundation – a
new creation in which all the principles were changed. These would evince
themselves by their new fruits – actions from new hopes & aims – and this
new creature would be in Christ Jesus – not in self – and to such and to
such only who walk by this rule could the Apostle or the Ministers of Christ
speak peace and mercy, for such only were the Israel of God. He urged most
[80] strongly on all not to judge of themselves by a comparison with others
they might deem less holy & so think themselves new creatures because in
their estimation there might be some worse, but to judge of themselves by
the unbinding righteous holy Law of God. And encouraging all to look to
God by earnest constant prayer & by searching the Scriptures to strive after a
change of heart which God has promised to give to all who by the spirit shall
ask it for Christ's sake. The Psalmody was mostly by the Youth in the Organ
Gallery, assisted by the Organ & scarcely at all by the Congregation.

The diarist is obviously pleased to find both the church service and the Sunday
school at Cromer well attended. He is also satisfied with the standard of the
service conducted by George Glover (later Archdeacon of Sudbury) who was
vicar of Cromer at this time. Nicknamed 'the Cardinal of Cromer' by one of
his opponents, this rather controversial man was the author of several pamphlets
including one entitled Observations on the Present State of Pauperism in England
(1817). Another nonconformist visitor, however, Simon Wilkin, wrote to a friend
in 1813, 'I never found a Sunday so dull on my hands before. Who preaches at
Cromer? Nobody Sir, only Mr Glover in the afternoon at Church.' Wilkin sums
up his derogatory remarks, ''tis not to me quite so agreeable to go to a little beggarly
uncomfortable damp church where only a few country folks are to be seen'.

The afternoon (Evening) service was attended equally numerously as that in the morning. The curate, Mr. Clews,[12] read the Prayers and Lessons with [81] a distinct voice – slowly & with a remarkable propriety. The Archdeacon was not one of the Congregation. The Revd. Mr. Henkinsson of Lynn Regis preach'd (read) a sermon of about 35 minutes from I Cor. I XVII: XVIII. "For Christ sent me not to baptize but to preach the Gospel not with wisdom of words lest the Cross of Christ should be made of none effect: for the preaching of the Cross is to them that perish foolishness; but unto us which are saved it is the power of God".

He shewed in the most plain and pleasing language what is to be understood by the Gospel of Christ. It is that which is designated by the Cross of Christ or his sufferings as a victim vicariously for those who believe – that this end being for Salvation shewed that all were sinners. That it ought to be a plain declaration of these glad tidings – to the expense of plainness not descending to vulgarity. That the wisdom [82] of words but obscured that which was too good to need much commending and always suffered when attempted to give it the ornament of wordy eloquence & this tended to counteract its efficacy. The Cross of Christ when plainly & truly preached was by the self-righteous then deemed foolishness – all natural pride was in arms against what was deemed the harsh severity of its condemnation, but when the spirit of God humbled the heart of a convinced sinner this preaching, in its very plainness, became the Power of God to Salvation. And then most plainly and sincerely & forcibly he urged his hearers not to deceive themselves but to examine closely whether even yet they had retired, and in secret from a broken heart, they had said when alone – God be merciful to me a sinner.

[83] Surely this church is privileged by such pulpit instruction – and the Congregations did themselves honor by the perfect stillness which prevailed & I believe by the attention paid to the Preacher.

Mr Fowell Buxton[13] and his Family were present both morning and afternoon.

A frequent visitor to Cromer was Sir Thomas Fowell Buxton, MP. Cromer Hall, owned by the Windham family, served the Buxtons as a holiday home from 1825 to 1828. When the family were searching for a new holiday residence, Richard Hanbury Gurney offered them Northrepps Hall, which he had purchased from the Barclays in 1795. Ellen and Richenda Buxton recorded in their diaries something of the hospitable atmosphere of these annual house parties – 'November 15 1862. When the Charles Buxtons were all here there were forty people sleeping in the house! And every day Maria, the cook, gets from Breese 18 large loaves of bread, and on Sunday she brings in more than 30!' 'July 12 1855. Beautiful weather. Our hay is going on, so we sent for the school children to play in it and an express to Cromer for plenty of strawberries and milk for their supper.'

Due in part to the work of such families, the influence of nonconformity was beginning to be felt in the area at about the time of the Martens' visit. The first application for a chapel in Cromer had come in 1819 from Henry Bedwell of Norwich. By 1823, applications had been made for Trunch, Knapton, Sidestrand, Trimingham, Mundesley and North Walsham.[14] Hannah Buxton reported with pride that 'The Bible and Missionary Societies were introduced and many efforts made for the good of the town', adding: 'Large crowds frequented our Sunday evening readings.'

### Monday the 19th September

**Weather pleasant but wind somewhat brisk. Walk'd Eastward on the sands about 1½ mile until stop'd by the HighWater and a large quantity of Cliff**

*Cromer from the east beach, showing recent erosion.*

which had fallen and prevented further progress until the sea should retire. Met here a very conversible Gentleman who with his son were seated on large Flints – the Father reading and the son improving his knowledge of Latin by studying in one of Dr. Valpy's publications.[15]

[84] When the Ebb permitted, the sands were resorted to by Gents & Ladies and Children: some pedestrians; others in Gigs: some in light carriages drawn by donkies: & some on Horseback. Among the latter were Mr Buxton and Dr Lushington.[16]

Read today from the newspaper the most dismal accident at the launching of the Queen Charlotte Man of War at Portsmouth by the bursting of the flood Gates & the consequent breaking of a Bridge crowded with Spectators and occasioning the loss of very many lives.[17]

Repeated the walk on the sands and saw the City of Edinburgh Steam Vessel pass us from Leith – & saw landed from her a large chest full [85] of Black Game from Scotland – alive & for Lord Walpole's[18] Orford preserve. His seat is near Wolterton & Mannington.

Tuesday 20th September

Weather still fine, wind s.w. & strong. Had a walk on the sands and then embarked in the Providence crab Boat for a little turn on the Ocean. As the tide was rising, the Master of the Boat carried the Ladies in his arms through the spreading wave to the Boat & then by watching the swells we got by little & little afloat. The wind was too strong off land to go far out to sea, but we kept within recovering distance, enjoying the lifting of the Billows as they passed under us.

[86] As we had to pull against both wind and tide we did not gain any great distance during the hour before we turned & when we did turn the wind & tide carried us back in half that time without any sail & scarcely with any aid from the Oars. The dancing on the sea was pleasant and was not attended with any tendency toward sickness. We felt the effect of the breakers on the shore a great deal more on landing than when putting off. We bought of the Master two large crabs (for 9 pence) which he had caught in the night and paid him 3/6 for his 1½ hours use of the Boat and his attendance & that of his son.

[87] The Steam Packet from London for Hull passed to day. There appeared very few Passengers on deck.

It is entertaining to see, while the wind is northerly or southerly & thus fair for the Colliers out & home, the many Vessels which are continually passing each other – those bound down all light & those bound to London all deeply laden. It put me in mind of the busy ants near their nest who all seem full of Life & activity & [are] often crossing each other – still making way so that none may be interrupted.

I returned Mr Buxton's call by waiting on him at Cromer Hall – an ancient looking building but large and surrounded by wood.[19] He has many Pheasants & some of the most beautiful plumage running about the grounds like [88] domestic fowls as he never suffers them to be shot or molested by fear.

Notice is given that the Cromer and East Norfolk Church Missionary Society's Anniversary will be held in the Cromer National School Room on Monday Evening next. It is pleasing to find such a spirit to promote the prosperity of the Kingdom of God prompting to activity and efficiency in all parts of the British Empire. May it ever increase & be its glory and the Crown of all its other honours!

*Cromer from the beach east of the lighthouse.*

# 5
# Norwich & Earlham

## Robert attends a great church gathering and dines at a quiet Quaker's home

[89] Wednesday the 22 September

Early this morning there came from the S.W. some heavy clouds which poured rain in large quantity & gave vivid lightning & close and loud thunder. These passed away over sea to the N.E. making our distant horizon in that quarter dark and dismal.

At 8 o'clock I mounted the coach Box and started for Norwich in some rain & expecting more. The country appeared highly cultivated & picturesque. Mr. R. Gurney, M.P. for Norwich, has well wooded ground and a comfortable residence.[1] Passed through North & South Repps, Trunch & other villages. The numerous churches here have formed a kind of common saying - Trimmingham, Gimmingham, [Knapton] and Trunch, NorthRepps & SouthRepps [lie] all in a Bunch. The grounds of Colonel Peters[2] are peculiarly [90] beautiful - fine pieces of water - a Parky Lawn - a good mansion - a lofty look-out Tower whence Yarmouth roads may be seen - a church in the midst of his woods - an Arch on the Road as a pointe de vue - extensive plantations of Firs & some noble Oaks. Lord Suffield also has some well covered grounds.[3] North Walsham Church Tower is in ruins - part - and great part, having fallen down not very long since. It is one of the

*Robert Marten's sketch of Trimingham church.*

square & flint built Church Towers common in this county. The Body of the Church is large & apparently in good repair & in use. This is a market Town & is well frequented on Thursday afternoons by Farmers for the Corn Trade.

The entrance into Norwich (about ¼ before 12, being about 25 miles) is by a poor & ill paved street.

[91] The Anniversary of the Auxiliary Bible Society[4] was held today in St. Andrew's Hall in which the Norwich Corn Market is also held. It was once a Monastery & has the appearance of a church. It is very large – I think equal to Guildhall in London. There are 52 paintings of considerable merit – in carved & gilt Frames, principally portraits of a succession of Mayors of the City – speakers of their Council, or of the City's representatives in Parliament. Those of Sir Harbord Harbord[5] (for which the corporation have been offered £600) – of the late Mr Windham[6] & the present William Smith[7] are conspicuously good. A large painting of Lady Jane Grey advancing to be beheaded & refusing the intreaties of the Catholics to die in the Roman Faith – & another of the same size of King Edward & the dying Eleanora[8] are by a young artist who was a native of Norwich & almost his only [92] productions & as he died young – he left these to the City. Admiral Lord Nelson's portrait is there.[9] At 1 o'clock the venerable Bishop [Bathurst] of Norwich now in his 81st year took the Chair in order to take his leave of public service to the society & to manifest to the last

his strong affection to its principles & management. He was received with great respect & supported by persons of eminence for piety and Talent – Mr Buxton M.P.[10] – the good Reverend Charles Simeon[11] of Cambridge – Reverend Mr. Cunningham[12] of Harrow – His Reverend Brother of Papfield [Pakefield] – Archdeacon Glover – Dr Johnson,[13] the friend of the poet Cowper, & the author of his "Life" – Mr Joseph Gurney of Earlham etc etc – Rev. Mr. Innes,[14] late of Camberwell, now of Norwich – Reverend Mr Alexander – Reverend Mr Sydney[15] & others. The attendance was about 800 persons, principally ladies. Mr Buxton, Mr Cunningham, Mr Glover, [93] Mr Innes & others spoke well & were very animated in the Bible cause. The Meeting ended at nearly 4 o'clock. Mr Buxton took me in his Phaeton[16] with several ladies to dine at Mr Joseph Gurneys at Earlham, about 2 miles west of Norwich. It is a large old House with spacious Rooms. The Hall has a fine collection of stuff'd Birds and other animals & the grounds are delightfully rural & extensive & being elevated command fine views of the country. He had invited (as usual at anniversary of the Bible Meeting) many & at half past 6 we sat down to an elegant dinner & in number 74 persons in one Room. After a short & silent pause Mr Gurney offered a few suitable words of prayer. When the cloth was removed, Mr Cunningham gave out the verse – "Praise God from whom all blessings flow etc" which was sung [94] by the whole company. The Ambassador, or accredited agent, from Mexico who had spoken at the Meeting then faced the company with further particulars relative to the willing reception of the word of God in that country – and Mr Cunningham gave an instance of the benumbing effects which an early dread of the informal Inquisition had on the mind of a sensible Catholic & whose energies though great could never so far conquer that dread as to be able to give his thoughts to the public nor his exertions for the general good. These elicited other remarks & with general & more particular conversation brought near to the hour of nine. To meet a wish which was mentioned, Paper & a pencil was handed round and each person at Table recorded his [95] or her name. Mr Cunningham then again requested the company & being permitted gave the following Hymn –

> Father whate'er of earthly Bliss
> Thy sovereign will denies
> Accepted at thy Throne of Grace
> Let this Petition rise

Give me a calm and thankful heart
From every murmur free
The blessings of thy Grace impart
And let me live to Thee
Let the sweet Hope that thou art mine
My Life and death attend
Thy presence on my Journey shine
And crown my Journey's end.

and which was sung with peculiar softness and great harmony of sound.

**When the Ladies had retired the conversation turn'd on the subject of the conduct of the Colonies and the sore [96] evils of Slavery – and the expediency of doing something to impress the public mind with these subjects now being on the very eve of a dissolution of Parliament – and the opinion that a County Meeting, if obtainable, would be one great & efficient mean as a public act & a good example to others. A meeting was agreed upon to confer on this matter at an early day.**

Returning to Norwich alone, Marten attends the anniversary meeting of the Auxiliary Bible Society at St Andrew's Hall. An 1842 guidebook claimed this building to be 'the largest and most splendid hall in the country devoted to municipal purposes'. The present structure was built in the fifteenth century by Sir Thomas Erpingham and his son, and once housed a community of Blackfriars. At the dissolution, the building was granted to the city, and the nave of the monastic church came to be used as a city hall. In 1776 the hall took on another function, as a corn exchange, one it retained until 1828.

The Norwich branch of the Auxiliary Bible Society had been established in 1811 by Joseph Kinghorn and Simon Wilkin, an occasion remarkable for being the first time a bishop of Norwich had appeared on the same platform as a dissenting minister. The diarist notes the respect paid to this bishop, Henry Bathurst, who was well known both as an advocate of liberal causes and for his unusual tolerance of dissenters. The 1842 Norwich Guide describes Bishop Bathurst as 'A worthy and much respected prelate, whose general benevolence, catholic spirit, Christian deportment, conciliatory manners, and extensive charity will long be remembered by the inhabitants of this city.'

After the meeting, as was customary, many of those present went to dine at Earlham Hall at the invitation of Joseph John Gurney (1788-1847). This annual gathering was hailed as 'the great religious festival of the county', and Earlham Hall as 'the resort of the wise and good of all denominations and of all ranks'.[17] In his memoirs the host recorded his own views of the 1825 dinner – 'It was particularly satisfying, pleasant and useful, without undue excitation.' Another guest recalled, 'We felt like the disciples on the Emmaus road', such was the atmosphere of the occasion.

Earlham Hall had been rented by the Gurneys from the Bacon family since 1786, and was their home for five generations. George Borrow, whose career Joseph John encouraged, remarked that 'the hall of many an earl lacks the bounty, the palace of many a prelate the piety & learning, which adorn the quiet Quaker's home.' The family of Gurney, or Gournay, who were said to have come to England with William I, played an important role in the religious and philanthropic life of England in the early nineteenth century. John Gurney, born in 1655, had connections with the Quaker sect, and it is possible that Puritan links existed before this. In Joseph John's lifetime the Gurneys were celebrated as one of the leading Quaker families in England, being intermarried with the Barclay family since 1752.

Although the Bible Society was said to have been one of Joseph John's chief interests, he was involved in many other ventures. Missionaries and agents were welcomed at Earlham, and one of his favourite projects was helping to distribute the Hebrew Scriptures amongst the Jews. Involved in the banking business established by his father in 1770, Joseph John claimed this was a constant source of trial to him, and that his worst cares arose out of being a 'monied man'. In a tribute to J. J. Gurney, Bishop Stanley remembered him as one 'whose peaceful life was one unwearied comment on evangelical charity at its fullest and most expanded state'.

Joseph John Gurney had become a Quaker minister at the age of 24 and, like his sister Elizabeth Fry, was actively involved in the anti-slavery campaign with his friend and brother-in-law Thomas Fowell Buxton. Conversation at the 1825 dinner turned naturally to this topical issue, and resulted in the formation of the 'Norwich Society for Promoting the Immediate mitigation and final Abolition of Slavery'.

**Tea was announced at 10 o'clock but many retired altogether at that hour. Many carriages were waiting – but being a moon-light night & quite fine, I walked back to the Hotel at Norwich in company with Mr Youngman[18] & my friends Alexander & Innes. The latter is now settled over a large church [97] in Norwich & much to his satisfaction.**

## Thursday 22 September 1825

After a good Breakfast I perambulated many of the streets of Norwich – looked in St. Stephen's Church[19] which is large and very handsome – is said to have been built in 1430 & is now in excellent repair. Passed the handsome Meeting House in Lady's Lane – having on it – St. Peter's Wesleyan Chapel[20] – and where sermons are to be preached next week – (and in another large Wesleyan Chapel)[21] – for the friends of the foreign Wesleyan Missions. I was also enabled to see at leisure the inside of the noble church of St. Peter in the market place,[22] also in fine order. The Bell was ringing for Morning Prayer but although the time was past, the Minister had not appeared & the Congregation in waiting was but one woman & two children.

[98] To day there was a Meeting in St. Andrew's Hall as an Anniversary of the Norwich Auxiliary Society for the Conversion of the Jews[23] & I estimated the number at about 500 Persons. A Mr. Bevan was in the Chair. I heard an encouraging report read & a speech from Mr Sydney and a part of a very affectionate & animating address from Mr Simeon but I could not stay longer, having to dine & to prepare to return at ½ past 3 o'clock by the Coach to Cromer & which place I reach'd before 8 o'clock.

From the late eighteenth or early nineteenth century Methodism was enjoying a period of growth in Norfolk.[24] John Wesley had first visited Norwich in 1754, renting a building known as the Foundry and establishing a Society. He soon took over the Tabernacle on Timber Hill, and a new chapel was built at Cherry Lane in 1769. By the early years of the nineteenth century the congregation had grown so large that one member described how 'every part of the chapel was crowded to excess and multitudes were obliged to go away for want of room.' Consequently, the Calvert Street and Lady Lane Chapels noted by the Martens were built to accommodate the demand for meeting places. From around 1820 most nonconformist chapels in Norfolk adopted a loosely classical architectural style, with pilasters, sash windows and symmetrical proportions being in evidence in those such as St Peter's described by the diarist as handsome.

# 6
# Back in Cromer

## Bracing winds, rusticity and respectability make the perfect health resort

My Ladies report that during my absence, the wind having increased, the sea had become somewhat turbulent. As this is the time for the equinoctial [99] Gales and it blows very freshly this Evening from the SouthWest, it is probable that by the time of HighWater tomorrow we may perceive still more of the effects of the now rising Gale.

This morning the Bell toll'd for the death of a Young Woman, an Inhabitant of Cromer who was well on Sunday but a corpse last Evening.


Friday the 23 September

Weather fine – wind at times inclinable to the North East – more at North West and came again to the South West.

Highwater to day about 4 o'clock. We walked round by Cromer Hall and mounted a Hill by a Path leading towards Felbrigg. This gave us [100] a pleasing view of the Country and of the sea over the woods which surround Cromer Hall. A large covey of Partridges passed us into those woods alarmed as we supposed by the frequent discharges from Fowling Pieces which we heard near to us & [which] were probably from a party of seven Gentlemen from the Hall.

*Mr Marten's sketch of Cromer from the south side, near Cromer Hall, on the way to Felbrigg.*

Thence we crossed some fields and wound our way up to the Light House and enjoyed again the view from that elevation and a little of the good conversation of the two old Ladies who reside there.

On our return we met Mr & Mrs Davis of Layton with their four children. Mrs D. had been sketching in the children's drawing Books & we had some amusement in our comparisons.

[101] We descended from the cliffs by the good staircase made from the grounds of the late Mr Hoare whose loss is greatly lamented here by the poor.[1] At different heights there are resting places & seats for four or five persons who may there commodiously read or converse or enjoy the full view of the wide expanse of waters. Hence the company on the sands are seen to advantage as they pass & the variety & the amusements of the children and the occupation of the Fishermen and sometimes of the men of the preventive service whose station and whose Boats are all very near afford objects for amusing observation.

The Life-Boat had been just fresh calk'd & got into good repair for winter service and is to day again on its carriage & ready for a start.

[102] The winds of the two or three past days have given much motion to the sea. At High Water the waves rolled to the shore with attractive grandeur, & when they broke on the Beach, lifting their enormous weights, and foaming when obstructed in their course, they dash'd furiously on the ground, and appeared as a mighty boiling caldron:- as in a mad confusion, till, forced by their own impulse up the inclined sands, they spread themselves a milk white sheet & returned to meet the wave which next succeeded.

Had our Evening walk on the Jetty amidst this pleasing scenery & enjoyed the roar of the Breakers while at times we felt the Jetty when struck by them tremble under us.

[103] Saturday 24 September

Weather still beautiful – wind fresh from the S.W. Walk'd on the sands westward about a mile to lower Runton.

Seeing some women & children busy on the sand & near to the retiring tide & at almost low ebb – made enquiry and was surprised to find their action in filling their Pails with fresh water which they conveyed across the broad sand

*Mrs Marten sitting on the steps of the cliff leading from Mr Gurney's house to the beach.*

to the Village on the Cliff for washing & other domestic purposes.[2] I tasted the water and found it perfectly fresh & of delightful taste. The women were dipping Basons into little pools in the sand which the sea had but just left & a spring through the sand kept the pool full. They then pointed [104] to my notice various places in the sand where the springs were bubbling up & these are much their dependence for fresh water – but they are not always to be had as these depend again a great deal on the state of the Earth & that on the supply from the clouds. These springs must come from deep as the cliffs are high, and the water does not rise through the sand but at a good distance from the cliff foot, & at a lower level. There were plenty of children & the women very civil. Hearing that the children went to school at twopence per week, we contributed to pay the schooling for a week or two, & left a little assortment of tracts which appeared to give a general satisfaction.

[105] We mounted the cliffs and were in our walk frequently hearing the sound of the discharge of fowling Pieces:- and soon discovered a youth attended by two servants & some dogs hunting a Hill well covered with Furze, & afterwards in a large turnip Field. The servant loaded the Piece, the other servant kept a lookout: the Dogs rummaged the cover, & the youth fired almost every ten minutes as the Dogs put up coveys in almost periodical succession, but the powder appeared to be wasted as the partridges generally got clear with only their fright – the young sportsman needing practice to make his shots tell. With the eagerness of the Dogs & the constant level for the destruction of the Birds I was reminded of the situation of poor David who, speaking of the enmity & the zeal of Saul and his servants, [106] complained that he was hunted "as a partridge on the mountains."

The Ladies could not withstand the temptation of the abounding Blackberries but gathered as they went 'till we reach'd upper Runton – a most desolate looking Boulderstone built & decaying place. One of the Porches of the Church is in ruins – but the inside appeared clean & well taken care of. It is large & some of the old fashioned Elm strong & carved seats or Benches for the poor still remain, but part is pewed. We were gratified to learn from an Old Man, very grey bearded, and who had been clerk (which he mentioned with a certain pride) that service is performed regularly every Sunday morning & that although the parish seemed so still & so dull & as if nearly uninhabited there was generally a Congregation of [107] between 200 and 300 people. We rested awhile in the Church Porch & as usual traversed the Burial Ground reading the Epitaphs and looking at ages of the persons when interred. We were pleased with the following warning admonition –

> "How vain is Life! Perhaps tomorrow's dawn
> O Reader! thou mayest never see.
> My fate will shew how slight a curtain's drawn
> Betwixt Eternity and Thee."

Many visitors to Cromer at this time took the trouble to walk towards Beeston and Sheringham and were rewarded with what Clement Scott later described as 'Exmoor-like' scenery. Louisa Hoare enjoyed walking along the Runton road, with its fields on one side and cliffs on the other. She delighted in the abundance of wild flowers, in particular the rare Vipers Bugloss, which turned the entire cliff top blue. Her diaries recall shooting parties in the woods around Cromer, and donkey drives to the Black Beacon for the spectacular views. Clement Scott claimed the view of this area from the Sheringham side as having 'the fairest prospect of distant sea and near foliage that ever delighted the picturesque sense.'[3]

**We walk'd back on nearly the edge of the lofty Cliffs enjoying the pleasing sight of the Ocean & many Vessels going both East and West with the off shore wind.**

**In our Evening walk on the Jetty we had a mild air – a smoothish sea – many well dressed persons – among the Gents were Lord Suffield & the Honourable Knox[4] – nearly a full moon silvering the waves, while nearly perpendicularly over the Light House whose 5 Lamps in united glare gave a Light remarkably differing from that of the larger luminary so highly elevated over it.**

The diarist's observation on the many 'well dressed' persons to be seen at Cromer once again testifies to the rather select atmosphere being deliberately fostered at this time. E. A. Goodwyn states that the influence of the large nonconformist families had much to do with the development of Cromer as an exclusive resort. One observer noted the absence of the 'adventurer', the 'fortune-hunter' and the 'blackleg' in its precincts. Although many visitors, like Marten, appreciated the quiet, respectable charms of Cromer, others complained of the lack of facilities. A visitor of 1823 reported that 'The want of public amusements is the universal complaint here and we are persuaded no bathing place can retain its visitors without them'.[5]

**[108] Another large Steam Vessel passed us today bound for London.**

**Sunday 25th September.**

A lovely morning – sea tranquil. Every thing Sabbath like – the Machines close up against the Cliffs – a few persons clean dressed on the sands and on the pier. Three French fishing Vessels came and anchored off the Town & their crews came on shore. These are the first of some hundreds of fishing Vessels which will be here in a few days to intercept the expected annual migration of Herrings. We were told that by the end of next week there will be visible from this place from 3 to 4 hundred such vessels each engaged to get as many as possible of this immense throng of these useful fish & that the fishing will continue from this coast as far as the north foreland in the British Channel.

Here again Marten shows his concern with propriety and respectability, this time regarding the observance of the Sabbath by Cromer visitors. Like many Georgian travellers he is pleased to be able to note the absence of bathing, the machines being high up on the sands. The atmosphere, in his view, is quiet and respectful, in keeping with a day of rest. An earlier visitor, Simon Wilkin, was rather less impressed with the town on a Sunday, stating 'This is a day with bathing people of little import: it is an old fashioned twelve hours which were much better out of the calendar. One is so dull; and tis not *right* to walk about so much as on other days'.

For the diarist, though, even on a Sunday there was plenty to do and see in Cromer without straying too far. The annual spectacle of the herring trawl coincided with his visit and provided some amusement. As Marten says, the three French boats were just the first of many to gather in September for the bumper catch. Yarmouth had similarly reaped the benefit of the herring migration for many years. In 1611 John Speed recorded 'there is yearly in September the worthiest herring fishery in Europe which draweth a great concourse of people, which maketh the town [Yarmouth] much the richer all the year following, but very unsavoury for the time.'

[109] At 11 o'clock the Church Bell summoned to the House of God – and the Avenues shewed a numerous throng of those who appeared willing Visitors. The Archdeacon read prayers and Mr Bickersteth[6.] preached from 96 Psalms 10–12 verses. His sermon was read & occupied 50 minutes of very interested attention. He adverted to the certainty of the prediction that God would judge – that is would govern his people – & in such circumstance as would come up to the happiness on which the Heaven and Earth are

called to rejoice. That the times gave signs of the approach of this glorious day. Associated energies of Christians were bringing about great effects. Mahommedans and Catholics manifested a fear which led to their taking steps to prohibit the reading of God's Holy Message. The Greek Church was receiving it in its purity. The Heathen had in a remarkable manner abandoned their Idols & turned to the living God. Christians had a growing concern for the Jews & the Jews manifested an unusual device to consider [110] the claims of Christianity. These signs were such that scarcely anything short of wilful blindness could overlook them & they called on real Christians to evince a still stronger decision of character – a greater energy in effort for the promotion of the more general coming of "the Kingdom of God & that His Will might be done upon Earth" – touching delicately yet with some emphasis on the high honor of our native country which is privileged to be the Treasurer to distribute the best riches to the Nations of the World.

At the close of the sermon – the 100th Psalm was sung – by the Lads in the Organ Loft – while the plate – a la mode du <u>continent</u> – was brought into each pew for the contributions of the Congregation, being presented to each individual for a donation or a refusal. This mode is, I think, novel, and being while in the professed act of [111] worshipping God by singing his praise, is open in my view to strong objections. The Collection amounted to £17.

The conduct of the Psalmody is, here, I think, scarcely justifiable. The Clerk names the number of the Psalm & gabbles rather than reads the two first lines – and three verses – & three verses only – are sung apparently without any regard to the sense – for it has happened in these two Sundays that the third, the concluding verse has ended in the middle of a subject so that in one place at the final word there was but a ; & in another not so much as a comma – yet ending the third verse the Organ ended and so did the Youths in the Loft and such of the Congregation below who had joined in this pleasing part of public worship – the part most akin to the worship in heaven.

Mr Clewes, the Curate, preached very acceptably in the afternoon from Ephesians, [112] from which he exalted the efficacy of the spirit of God in his influence on the human mind – debated Man's pride – magnified the privilege & advantage and exhorted to the duty of Prayer – pressed the necessity of being rooted & grounded in the love of the Lord – to a very attentive auditory. At the conclusion of the service he baptized a Child and then attended at the grave of the young female already mentioned, during which latter service the Burial Ground was lined with people and the windows of the Houses near the Churchyard had many observers.

In the Evening Mr Clewes familiarly addressed the Children of a National School[7] – heard them repeat what they had learned from the Scriptures & collects[8] & these he afterwards very plainly [113] and very suitably to their capacities explained & urged upon their practice. There were many of the inhabitants present & Mr Clewes closed the hour by a beautiful extempore Prayer.

Among other things he warned them against being laughed or scorn'd out of their religion or integrity of principle by wicked Boys or wicked Men. These, he said, could but laugh or revile but could not hurt. They might call them Methodists but they would do them no harm & of this they ought not to be ashamed. If they were ashamed of God & of his reproach, God might be hereafter ashamed of them, & that would, in the end be most woful. He had read to the Boys the Life of Thomas Mann the honest waterman,[9] & was glad to hear that I knew him, and could vouch for its truth.

## [114] Monday 26 September

Morning hazy – wind much abated & a large fleet of loaded Colliers going to the Southward. Two Brigs beach'd to discharge coals at Cromer. The Children who were at the school last night were at Mr Davis' Door by his appointment as he had promised those present sixpence each because of their attendance at the school.

Edmund Bartell remarked in his guide that despite the lack of a convenient harbour at Cromer there were small imports and exports of coal, tiles, oil-cake, and London porter into the town. The necessity of unloading the coal from ships and dragging it up the beach in carts meant that complaints were often heard about the high prices. The sight of ships being unloaded on the beach continued to provide entertainment for visitors, though, until the advent of the railways in the 1880s, the last cargo of coal being unloaded on the beach in March 1887.

Cromer is surrounded by a very pleasant hilly Country and by Villages to which there are rural walks. The Light House is a great ornament, as from its height it is seen from almost every point. There are good Country Houses near it & the neighbourhood is very respectable. Itself is quite a [115] rustic place with few shops and those quite country fashion – very little inticement to spend money. There is a shop with such wares as are usually found in what are called at watering places Libraries,[10] but no Evening meetings there. There are few Lodgings with views of the sea, although there are commodious Lodgings very near to it – excepting however a Row of new Houses built purposely to let for short periods & which command good sea views.[11] The Houses are all (but the new ones) built of Flint Boulder stones & a few Bricks. The church is conspicuous from every point. Fish not plenty except Lobsters which, and large crabs which may always be had and the first are sometimes brought to Table hot as a first course. The articles of Butchers meat are few & cannot always be had, but wild Rabbits which are good may be obtained.

[116] The Inhabitant poor are very civil & not one beggar appeared. It is upon the whole a pleasant retirement with a good air, a noble sea, much traffick constantly in sight either near or distant, and having the Gospel preach'd in the Church, has many attractions for those whose aim in their excursion is benefit in health by Air & relaxation and who can be content without being in the midst of a multitude of Holiday Makers whenever they leave their door.

Of the New Inn & their obliging Landlord (whom we left confined to bed by the Gout) & Landlady & their most civil and attentive Daughters – of the fare & cleanliness of the House and of the ready attention of the servants it is but a justice due to them to speak in their praise.

Cromer obviously suited the needs of the Marten family perfectly, with its refined gentility, its pretty walks, and its bracing sea air. They were certainly not the only visitors to recognise the health-giving properties of a Cromer holiday. Jane Austen discussed the merits of Cromer in *Emma* (1814), advising, 'You should have gone to Cromer my dear, if you went any where. Perry was a week at Cromer once, and he holds it to be the best of all sea bathing places. A fine open sea, he says, and very pure air'. Even in 1904 the *Daily News* was recommending, 'For robust mortals wishful to be even more robust Cromer is the place . . . Your lungs are strengthened by air blowing pure and unadulterated from the North Pole'.

# 7

# Norwich to London

## Georgian delights and country living

[117] We left Cromer by the Coach at 8 [in the] morning. The Coach with four inside & 16 outside & with plenty of Baskets – Game – Trunks – Bags, etc etc. Saw both Partridges & pheasants as we travelled & saw our sportsman put up 10 of the former close to us, and miss all, though he fired at them at a small distance. We arrived at Norwich and left the Norfolk Hotel in an excellent chaise in which we were rattled to the Cock Inn at Attleborough by a pleasant road in less than two Hours. Attleborough is a Market Town. Walk'd round the burial Ground & noticed the odd epitaphs & the attempts at serious Rhymes which appear in country church yards. Those in the little cemetery of the little Baptist Chapel were far superior – good & well chosen quotations from valuable authors. We took refuge in the Chapel during a sudden shower. There were four women only & whom we supposed to have met for prayer. The church is large, ancient, and noble.

[118] Our Friend Mr J. F.[1] lives three miles wide of the High Road. The House is named Hockham Lodge where we were received with affectionate attention. We dined at half past 6 o'clock with every Table Comfort. The Clergyman of the Parish of Shropham dined with us, but Mr L., son of Sir Thomas L.,[2] was prevented by having caught the Ague[3] from exposure to the Rain outside a Stage Coach. After Tea we conversed 'till the usual hour for family prayer when all the Domestics entered the Drawing Room and the

Reverend Mr Beever[4] read from a publication by Mr Pearson[5] the prayers for the Evening. Mr. F. mention'd the pleasing effects which Family Prayers had produced in his man servant who [119] a swearer – a Drinker & a quareller became the contrary & thus instead of dismissing him as he had once intended, he now found him valuable and trustworthy.

Mr F. & the clergyman are both good shots – and on their invitation I accompanied the Gamekeeper on their going out the next morning – the duties of the family having been first seriously performed, the prayers being read with solemnity by Mr B. Mr F. has in the whole twenty Dogs – Pointers – Terriers & Greyhounds. Smack & Venus were selected to do the duties of the Field and they appeared not only able for but delighted with that Duty. Mr F. was so equipped for the hard labor & the expected occurrences of the Field that assuredly I [120] could not have recognized him as the Gentleman I had dined with the preceding Evening had he not been on his own premises & other circumstances leading to that conclusion. The produce of the two Guns during the day was 29 Partridges, 1 Hare, & 1 Rabbit – the latter was given to a working man in the Field. To me this was a novel sight. The docility of the Dogs was very noticeable. They obeyed the motion of the hand as to which way they were to go to search the Field – upon either Dog pointing – the other stopped wherever he saw his Master's hand lifted up

*Mr Marten made two sketches of Hockham Lodge.*

as a signal – neither stirred till the covey was sprung & the pieces fired – & then the Dogs watched to see if any fell & went to fetch the fallen Bird – or if the Master saw, & the Dog did not see, & [121] the Master said Hie! Lost! – the Dog immediately set out in the way which the Birds went off – and if the Master found – the words Hie! Found! would at once bring the Dogs back – and while the pieces were being reloaded – the Dogs were quite still, waiting for a waive of the Master's hand to renew their hunt of discovery.

I returned after an hour or two, but the Gentlemen continued between four and five hours & in this their sport (so called) they journeyed on foot somewhat encumbered with powder, shot and Fowling piece more than twenty miles over ploughed land & through stubble & tall sweedish turnips & potatoes – getting through hedges & over Banks, & this almost daily for amusement – continued either in shooting or coursing from the first of September 'till the last of March.

[122] Of course we dined again at a very fashionable hour. The Evening was spent partly in reading & conversing & on the servants retiring from the Family Meeting – The retirement of the whole for the night appeared as by general consent. The produce of Mr F. and his friends Guns on his Manor last season was 1054 head of Game. These Guns are fired by percussion, and as I had never before seen a lock on that principle I fell interested in the examination. Partridges are very numerous, and are found especially among the turnips to which they resort for cover.

On the Wednesday a party was made for a ride & Mrs F. drove the Gig in which she took Mrs M. The Reverend rode Mrs F's saddle horse & the convalescent Mr L. [123] rode White Peter. Our first visit was near to Mr B.'s church at Shropham now under repair. The Congregation since he became the Curate has greatly increased and some poor people with whom I conversed gave him a very approving word as a good Young Man who made their duty plain by his plain preaching. Mrs F., Sarah & self walked to the Church and the Equestrians with the Ladies went round by Lallingford [Larlingford]. Mrs F. entertained us in the Evening with her performance on the Harp whose strings she swept with boldness and with a Master's Art.

We received from Mr & Mrs F. every possible kindness & especially from the amiable & delicate & continued attentions of the latter whose good management – affability & elegant manners contributed much to our comfort.

*Hockham Lodge*

[124] **The House is built with large gravel stones like the Boulderstone buildings[s] and has been very much improved in its interior & more in the grounds by Mr F. who works hard in his garden and has much taste for these improvements. And he looks to every thing himself & mostly lends his own hand to expedite while he directs the performance.**

Hockham Lodge belonged not to the Hockham, but to the Shropham estate owned by the Hemsworth family. The Lodge itself was probably built around 1805 as a gentleman's residence, and at one time was the home of the agent of the estate. At the time of the Martens' visit the house was owned by Rev. George Reading Leathes, who had married Sarah Hemsworth in 1813, who presumably rented the property to tenants. Leathes was a respected botanist who had contributed to *English Botany* published in 1823 and had a genus of seaweed named after him. He also donated specimens to Norwich Castle Museum, which began life in 1825 as part of the Norfolk and Norwich Literary Institution.

In this setting the diarist and his family enjoy the diverse pleasures of Georgian country living, including shooting, riding and a musical evening. J. H. Plumb claims in his book *Georgian Delights* that people travelled at this time to be morally uplifted, as well as to satisfy their curiosity over how others lived, particularly those richer than themselves. A. Tinniswood goes further in *The Polite Tourist* and suggests that by noticing and approving, the visitor could share in the owner's statement of culture and taste. Mr Marten is obviously impressed with some aspects of his friend's lifestyle, especially with his good taste in the fashionable pursuit of landscape gardening, and with the institution of family prayer.

Although he marvels at the well-trained pointers, a breed recently developed for shooting, the guest appears less keen than his host on this 'so called' *sport*. Hunting was the most popular rural sport in this period, with shooting suffering from the restrictions of complex game laws. Sale of game was also forbidden by law and it could only appear on the table as a gift which meant that organised poaching and selling flourished. Before the revolutionary invention of the percussion cap in 1807 enabling the faster and safer loading of guns, the sport used cumbersome flintlock weapons.

Music was another fashionable diversion of country living which was becoming increasingly popular in the Georgian era with the availability of cheaper instruments after 1750. The Georgian gentleman would also be well fed with locally supplied meat, fish and game, accompanied by fresh seasonal fruit and vegetables, as well as imported luxuries. Dinner time in England gradually got later and later from early afternoon, and by this time was usually around 6.30 or 7. Country houses began to serve an informal meal called luncheon to bridge the gap between breakfast and dinner, often eaten by ladies, the gentlemen being occupied with their field sports.

**We left this hospitable Family on Thursday Morning – having heard there of the death of my Brother-in-Law Mr. J. Giles of Gravesend in order to attend his interrment.**

**On changing Horses at Thetford I was spoken to by name by a Gentleman whom I did not know but who thanked me for a service rendered him [125] long ago by a letter of introduction at Smyrna where he went out as a missionary to Asia. His name was Cooke & he had but just returned.**

**We passed through Newmarket & put up at the Sun Inn at Cambridge & after some refreshment viewed the Kings College Chapel, the Trinity College Library & its chapel. All very worthy of notice for their respective beauties & curiosities – and especially in the latter, the Statue of Sir Isaac Newton by the celebrated Roubiliac[6] – as lecturing on the qualities & nature of Light & the results of the refraction by the Prism which he appears holding in his hand.**

We observed some confusion in the Inn and were induced to make enquiry
– when we learned [126] that the Master who had been ill of a fever brought
on probably by fretting under some disappointments & what he thought evil
prospects had cut his throat in his kitchen – possibly in a state of delirium!

Our Friends at Melbourne gave us their accostomed kind welcome. The
widow! – exerted herself for our hospitable entertainment:- but the death of
Mr Carver[7] has made a visible vacuum in that happy Family.

We left Melbourne on Friday morning at ½ past 9 by the Tally Ho! Coach
and were safe at the Bell Inn Aldgate by ¼ past 2 – & at Plaistow by 7 all well
& we trust thankful.

[127] The celebrated Captain Barclay the Pedestrian accompanied me on
the coach-top from Cromer to Norwich. His young daughter was inside the
coach.

After a brief stop in Cambridge spent visiting some of the colleges, the family
depart for home having heard of the death of Mr Giles. The journey ends on
another sad note, with the suicide of Mr Carver, proprietor of the Sun Inn.
Leaving Cambridge on Friday 30th September the Martens complete their long
and eventful excursion aboard the *Tally Ho* coach, no doubt satisfied that their
journey for health and pleasure has achieved its desired results.

It is perhaps fitting that the last fellow traveller Robert Marten mentions
in his journal was one of the greatest athletes of his time, a man who similarly
sought adventure for health and pleasure, but also for fame and fortune. The
Georgian era was full of stories of trials of strength and stamina, and people
were obsessed with sport and gambling. It is perhaps no wonder that such a
man as Robert Barclay Allardice, who made his name by winning a bet for
a thousand guineas to walk a thousand miles in a thousand hours, should
achieve celebrity status. It is also a feature of the idiosyncrasy of the Georgian
era that despite advances in coach transport and the innovation of steam,
some people still preferred to travel by foot and to prove themselves by such
marathon effort.

# Appendix

The following extracts are from family papers which are part of a collection held in the Genealogy Center of the Allen County Public Library, Indiana, USA. The series consists of the family memoirs of T. W. Powell, who married a granddaughter of Robert Marten and worked in Canada and the US from the 1850s onwards. Amongst the papers can be found letters and autobiographical material which throw new light on the character of Robert Marten, in particular the extent of his travels and journals and his great sense of humour and love of playing with his grandchildren.

## Letters of Charles Marten to his father Robert Marten 1822

The young man writes of his 'indulgent father' and begs him to make his health and not his journal the object of his tour, advising that he needs to build his strength to tackle his roses. A light diet and some wine, but no 'bilious malt liquor' is recommended, along with sound sleep and the avoidance of late night writing and thinking. Charles talks of the sound advice and sense of Robert's wife Emma and the interest she takes in the welfare of the whole family. He also recalls the 'careful' education he and his siblings received at home.

## Extracts from the autobiography of Mary Marten (the wife of T. W. Powell)

Mary remembers her grandfather as a very clever man who had an untiring ability and much clear-sightedness in business. He knew how to use opportunities of advancement well, and to create them for himself. He had a genial nature, a warm heart, plenty of broad humour and considerable public spirit. When he had made his considerable fortune, she writes, Robert gave up the drudgery of business and devoted himself to a variety of Christian and philanthropic schemes. He wrote voluminous journals of his many travels abroad and at home, illustrated with rough but expressive sketches.

Mary remembers him as an old man, and she was 13 when he died –

> He was a very fine old gentleman . . . large, indeed corpulent, but very active, with a fine bold forehead fringed by very silvery hair'. Robert had inherited his 'courtly' manners from his father, but his long acquaintance with the world had given him a 'very racy mother-wit, which caused him to be exceedingly entertaining to us children'. In old age he still went to London in his carriage every day as he continued to hold the directorships of several boards long after giving up business. Sometimes he would invite the grandchildren to accompany him which they considered a huge treat as 'he would joke and play with us nearly all the way.

Robert was very generous, in both gifts and hospitality, Mary recalls, and so he did not die as rich as commonly expected. She particularly remembers being given a very large doll called Emily who was furnished with several outfits, as well a book of verse written especially for her by her grandfather. Robert took great pleasure in arranging and writing instructive lectures for the villagers on various subjects which he would read in the schoolroom on one evening every week. At Christmas, despite being a dissenter, he would attend church in the morning and invite the minister and his wife to dine with the family. After the meal the younger children would take great delight in trying to catch the older family members in an energetic game of *Blind Man's Buff*.

# Notes

## Introduction

1. J. Walvin, *English Urban Life 1776–1851* (1984)
2. J. Richardson, *The Regency* (1973)
3. L. Cooper, *The Age of Wellington* (1963)
4. A. Bryant, *The Age of Elegance* (1950)
5. J. Walvin, *English Urban Life 1776–1851* (1984)
6. J. Clarke, *The Price of Progress* (1977)
7. J. Walvin, *English Urban Life 1776–1851* (1984)
8. J. Walvin, *English Urban Life 1776–1851* (1984)
9. J. Walvin, *English Urban Life 1776–1851* (1984)
10. H. Perkin, *The Origins of Modern English Society* (1969)
11. I. Campbell Bradley, *Enlightened Entrepreneurs* (1987)
12. J. Richardson, *The Regency* (1973)
13. J. Richardson, *The Regency* (1973)
14. J. Simmons, *Journeys in England* (1951)

## 1 London to Great Yarmouth

1. Register ton – a unit of internal capacity in ships.
2. Wherry – a half-covered commercial boat.
3. B. Greenhill & A. Giffard, *Victorian and Edwardian Merchant Steamships from old photographs* (1979)
4. Tried Corner Stone – Isaiah 28:16 'Therefore thus saith the Lord GOD, Behold, I lay in Zion for a foundation stone, a tried stone, a precious corner stone, a sure foundation: he that believeth shall not make haste'.
5. Weal – prosperity, wellbeing. Obsolete uses: the state, wealth.
6. Grog – diluted spirit, especially rum, from 'Old Grog', Edward Vernon, a British admiral who issued diluted rum, and whose nickname was derived from

the grogram cloak he wore, grogram being a coarse fabric.

7.   C. R. Vernon Gibbs, *British Passenger Liners of the Five Oceans* (1963).

8.   Possibly Sheerness, off the Kent coast, or Shoeburyness, off the Essex coast.

9.   Leeward – the sheltered side of a ship.

10.  Videlicet – namely.

11.  Larboard – a former nautical term for port.

12.  Walton-on-the-Naze – an impressive beacon with an octagonal brick tower was built here in 1720.

13.  Landguard – a fortress that stands at the mouth of the river Orwell, built in the seventeenth century.


## 2  Great Yarmouth

1.   Gorleston and Southtown are now in Norfolk, but before the 1970s county boundary changes they were in Suffolk.

2.   The first drawbridge in Yarmouth had been built in 1427 and linked the centre of the quay with the west side of the river Yare. It was subsequently rebuilt in 1553, 1570 and 1809.

3.   Alan Thrower.

4.   The mizen sail is set on a 'mizenmast', either on the aftermast or on the third sail, depending on the size of the vessel. A lugsail is a four-sided sail suspended from a yard.

5.   Gorleston's Dutch pier, constructed during the sixteenth century.

6.   T. West Carnie, *In Quaint East Anglia* (1899).

7.   The General Steam Navigation Company ran steamers from London Bridge Wharf to Yarmouth, Margate, Southend, etc.

8.   Regent Street – opened in 1813 at a cost of £30,000, the great expense being due to the cost of purchasing and removing buildings. Chapel Street – now known as King Street, was named after St George's Chapel built there in 1715.

9.   The river Waveney.

10.  The Norfolk wherry – a trading vessel unique to the Broads, ideal for sailing the narrow rivers, being long and low, shallow keeled, with one huge square sail.


## 3  Norwich

1.   The Norfolk Hotel, Broad Street, St Giles.

2.   Lath – expanded sheet metal or wire mesh used to provide backing for plaster or rendering.

3.   M. H. Wilkin, *Joseph Kinghorn of Norwich* (1855).

4.   R. Hale, 'Nonconformity in Nineteenth Century Norwich' in *Norwich in the Nineteenth Century*, ed. C. Barringer (1984).

5.   S. C. Colman, quoted by R. Hale, 'Nonconformity in Nineteenth Century Norwich'.

6.   R. Hale, 'Nonconformity in Nineteenth Century Norwich'.

7.   J. Alexander, *Thirty Years' History of the Church and Congregation in Prince's Street* (1847).

8.   *Norwich Spectator* (1862), quoted by R. Hale, 'Nonconformity in Nineteenth Century Norwich'.

9.   Constructed by Boulton & Watt at their factory near Birmingham.

10.   Built on the Denes in 1818 and considerably enlarged in 1825 to employ 700 people.

11.   J. K. Edwards, 'Industrial development 1800–1900' in *Norwich in the Nineteenth Century*, ed. C. Barringer (1984).

12.   J. K. Edwards, 'Industrial development 1800–1900'.

13.   Fastnesses – fortifications for a stronghold or fortress.

14.   G. K. Blyth, *The Norwich Guide* (1842).

15.   Millbank Penitentiary, built in 1813–21 in an area sometimes known as Chelsea at this time.

## 4 Cromer

1.   The picturesque countryside at Thorpe at this time enjoyed a reputation as the 'Richmond of Norfolk', being much favoured by local artists and wealthy gentlemen in search of a summer retreat.

2.   On 19th July 1825 *The Times* reported, 'The effects of the continued hot weather begins to be very seriously felt.' Cattle and crops were suffering, horses dying in the streets, and reports of human fatalities soon followed.

3.   The New Inn and the King's Arms Hotel in Garden Street were the only sizeable inns before the Hotel de Paris opened in 1830.

4.   Probably Edmund Bartell's *Cromer Considered as a Watering Place* (1806).

5.   Mid-Victorian trade directories showed that Cromer supported two gemstone dealers, a jeweller and a shop selling seashells.

6.   Resembling soap, soapy. Cromer is built on a ridge of glacial sands and gravels.

7.   Samuel Hoare (1783–1847), MP, the London banker and philanthropist who owned Cliff House, Cromer.

8.   According to Verily Anderson, there were at one time 16 sizeable houses in the area inhabited by these large families, plus several holiday cottages in Cromer and Northrepps.

9.   Clement Scott, *Poppyland* (1886).

10. Edward Harbord (1781–1835) 3rd Baron Suffield, MP, a zealous advocate for the abolition of slavery and a great prison reformer.

11. The Sunday School Society was founded in 1785. By the end of the eighteenth century both the Church of England and the dissenting sects were setting up Sunday Schools with the main aim of teaching children to read the Bible.

12. Possibly Rev. Thomas Clowes.

13. Sir Thomas Fowell Buxton (1786–1845), MP, the famous philanthropist and prison reformer, nicknamed the 'Liberator of the slaves' through his leadership of the campaign to abolish slavery in British Colonies.

14. E. A. Goodwyn, *Cromer Past* (1980).

15. Edward Valpy (1764–1832) headmaster of the Norwich School, whose *Elegantiae Latinae* (1803) went into ten editions during his own lifetime.

16. Stephen Lushington (1782–1873), lawyer, ardent anti-slavery campaigner, and staunch churchman.

17. The 1825 *Annual Register* records the tragic launching of the *Queen Charlotte*, the largest ship ever built at Portsmouth, with the loss of 16 lives.

18. Horatio Walpole (1783–1858), 4th Earl of Orford, whose seat was Wolterton Hall, near Aylsham.

19. The Hall described by Marten was rebuilt in the late 1820s in Gothic revival style by William Donthorn.

## 5 Norwich

1. Northrepps Hall, the home of Richard Hanbury Gurney MP.

2. Westwick Park, the setting for John Petre's residence built by John Berney in the reign of Queen Anne.

3. Gunton Hall, the seat of the Suffield family, built in 1785.

4. The Bible Society was formed with the aim of distributing the Scriptures to Sunday Schools and missionaries.

5. Sir Harbord Harbord MP, first Baron Suffield, whose portrait was painted by Gainsborough.

6. William Windham MP (1784–1802), who was known for his fair-minded, frank and generous nature. His portrait was painted by Hoppner in 1803.

7. William Smith MP (1802–30), dissenter and radical, friend of Wilberforce and supporter of the campaign to abolish slavery. Portrait by Thompson.

8. Painted in 1787 by a young artist called Martin.

9. Painted by Sir William Beechey in 1800 following victory over Spain.

10. Sir Thomas Fowell Buxton MP; see note 12 to section 4.

11. Rev. Charles Simeon, Fellow of King's College, Cambridge, and highly influential minister of Trinity Church.

12. Rev. John William Cunningham, evangelical minister, whose brother, Rev. Francis Cunningham, married Richenda Gurney in 1816.

13. Rev. John Johnson (died 1833), the friend and distant relative of the poet William Cowper. Rector of Yaxham 1800–33. Author of *Sketch of the Life of Cowper* (1815).

14. Rev. John Boutet Innes (died 1837), who became pastor of the Independent Old Meeting House, Norwich in November 1825, having moved from Weymouth in 1824.

15. Possibly the E. Sidney at whose house in Norwich an annual meeting of the Bible Society was held.

16. A light four-wheeled, horse-drawn carriage, usually with two seats.

17. Quoted by R. Hale in *Norwich in the Nineteenth Century* ed. C. Barringer (1984).

18. William Youngman, a Suffolk businessman who set up as a wine merchant in Norwich and later went into business with Simon Wilkin as a bookseller.

19. Situated at the west end of Rampant Horse Street; built after the Reformation.

20. Situated in Bethel Street, opened in 1824, seating 1,000.

21. Calvert Street Chapel opened in 1811, seating 1,050.

22. St Peter Mancroft, begun in 1430, finished in 1455.

23. Founded in 1809.

24. J. Ede, *Halls of Zion* (1994).


## 6 Back in Cromer

1. Samuel Hoare (1751–1825), the wealthy Quaker banker of Paradise Row, who married Sarah Gurney of Keswick. In a memoir of Samuel, his widow recalls how he was 'known to every person in Cromer and universally beloved for he was the friend and comforter of all'.

2. Water supply in this period was still erratic, water being pumped from wells or obtained by storing rainwater.

3. Clement Scott, *Poppyland* (1886).

4. Possibly Admiral the Hon. Edmund Knox (1787–1867), Speaker in the Irish House of Commons.

5. E. A. Goodwyn, *Cromer Past* (1980).

6. Rev. Edward Bickersteth (1786–1850) who was described as a 'terrible Methodist' before taking orders in the Anglican Church.

7. Schools set up by the National Society for Church of England Schools, established in 1811, were known as National Schools and supported by the parish churches. The school in Cromer, supported by the Goldsmiths' Company, had recently been reorganised along National Society lines.

8. Short prayers, generally preceding the lesson.

9. No. 249 of the Religious Tract Society's tracts: *The Honest Waterman; or, Some Account of the Life and Character of Thomas Mann.*
10. Bartell mentions a small circulating library consisting of a few novels.
11. Possibly the Crescent built on the East Cliff shortly before 1823.


## 7 Norwich to London

1. Joshua Finch is named as an occupier of Hockham Lodge in 1825 and listed in White's 1845 directory as a farmer.
2. Possibly Sir Thomas Loveday.
3. Fever.
4. Possibly the same Rev. Thomas Beevor, a neighbour of Parson Woodforde, who was imprisoned in 1801 for challenging Captain Pain to a duel.
5. Edward Pearson (1756-1811), a Norwich-born theologian, the author of many publications, including *Prayers for Families.*
6. James Giles, who was the brother of Robert's second wife's sister, died on 25th September and was buried on 1st October.
7. Louis Francois Roubiliac (1705-62), who came to England around 1732, exhibiting his statue of Newton in 1755.
8. In his autobiography the diarist refers to a 'Reverend William Carver of Melburne Cambridgeshire' to whom he sent his sons for education, and who was possibly related in some way to the landlord of the Sun Inn.

# Bibliography

## Historical background

Anderson, J. & Swinglehurst, E., *The Victorian and Edwardian Seaside* (1978)

Bradley, I. C., *Enlightened Entrepreneurs* (1987)

Brander, M., *The Georgian Gentleman* (1973)

Briggs, A. (editor), *The Nineteenth Century* (1985)

Bryant, A., *The Age of Elegance 1812–1822* (1950)

Clarke, J., *The Price of Progress* (1977)

Cobbett, W., *Rural Rides* (1830)

Cooper, L., *The Age of Wellington* (1963)

Gauldie, E., *Cruel Habitations: A History of Working Class Housing 1780-1918* (1974)

Glover, M., *Wellington's Army* (1977)

Harvey, A. D., *Britain in the Early Nineteenth Century* (1978)

Horn, P., *Life and Labour in Rural England* (1987)

Jarrett, D., *England in the Age of Hogarth* (1974)

Norman, E. R., *Church and Society in England 1770–1970* (1976)

Parreaux, A., *Daily Life in England in the Reign of George III* (1966)

Perkin, H., *The Origins of Modern English Society* (1969)

Plumb, J. H., *Georgian Delights* (1980)

Radford, P., *The Celebrated Captain Barclay* (2001)

Richardson, J., *The Regency* (1973)

Rouse, M., *Coastal Resorts of East Anglia* (1982)

Thompson, D. M., *Nonconformity in the Nineteenth Century* (1972)

Walvin, J., *Beside the Seaside* (1978)

Walvin, J., *English Urban Life 1776–1851* (1984)

Williams, E. N., *Life in Georgian England* (1962)

## Travel

Barber, P. (editor), 'Journal of a Traveller in Scotland 1795–96' in Scottish Historical Review, 36 (1957)

Boswell, J., Journey of a Tour to the Hebrides 1740–1793 (1785)

Brereton, O. S., Observations in a Tour through South Wales, Shropshire, etc. (Read at the Society of Antiquaries, February 13, 1772) (1775)

Bruyn Andrews, C. (editor), The Torrington Diaries (1954)

Burton, A. & P., The Green Bag Travellers: Britain's First Tourists (1978)

Clifford, J. L., Hester Lynch Piozzi (1941)

Clifford, J. L. (editor), Dr Campbell's Diary of a Visit to England in 1775 (1947)

Cobbett, W., Rural Rides, 1830

Cox, E. G., A Reference Guide to the Literature of Travel, Vol. 3 (1949)

'Diary of their Majesties Journey to Weymouth and Plymouth', Gentleman's Magazine, No.68 (1789)

Gray, A. (editor), Papers and Diaries of a York Family 1764–1839 (1927)

Hibbert, C. (editor), An American in Regency England (1968)

James, P. (editor), The Travel Diaries of T. R. Malthus (1966)

Johnson, S., A Journey to the Western Islands of Scotland (1773)

Ketton-Cremer, R. W., The Early Life and Diaries of William Windham (1930)

Mann, E. (editor), An Englishman at Home and Abroad (1930)

Moritz, C., Travels of Carl Philipp Moritz in England 1782 (1924)

Raistrick, A. (editor), The Hatchett Diary (1967)

Riviere, M., 'The Rev William Gunn: A Norfolk Parson on the Grand Tour', Norfolk Archaeology, 33 (1965)

Simmons, J. (editor), Journeys in England (1951)

Tinniswood, A., The Polite Tourist (1989)

Wilberforce, W., Journey to the Lake District from Cambridge 1779 (1983)

Withey, L., Cooks Tours: A History of Leisure Travel 1750 to 1915 (1997)


## Local history

Alexander, J., Thirty Years History of the Church and Congregation in Princes Street Chapel (1847)

Alexander, W., Memoir of the Rev J. Alexander (1856)

Anderson, V., The Northrepps Grandchildren (1968)

Barclay, O., Thomas Fowell Buxton and the Liberation of Slaves (2001)

Barringer, C. (editor), Norwich in the Nineteenth Century (1984)

Bartell, E., Cromer Considered as a Watering Place (1806)

Blyth, G. K., The Norwich Guide (1842)

Braithwaite, J. B., *Memoirs of Joseph John Gurney*, Vol.1 (1902)

Browne, *History of Congregationalism in Norfolk and Suffolk* (1877)

Creighton, R. G., *Ellen Buxton's Journal* (1967)

Eade, P., *Some Account of the Parish of St. Giles, Norwich* (1886)

Eade, P., *The Norfolk and Norwich Hospital* (1900)

Ede, J., Virgoe, N. & Williamson, T., *Halls of Zion: Chapels and Meeting-Houses in Norfolk*, Centre of East Anglian Studies (1994)

Goodwyn, E. A., *Cromer Past* (1980)

Grose, J.R., *Cromer: These were Their Days* (1999)

*A Guide to Cromer . . . by a visitor* (1851)

Hall, B., 'From the pages of an 1837–40 diary', *North Norfolk News* 29th August (1952)

Hare, A. J. C., *The Gurneys of Earlham* (1845)

Hedges, A., 'Yarmouth Inns – Their Signs and Associations', *Norfolk Fair* (1972)

Jewson, C. B., *The Baptists in Norfolk* (1957)

Jewson, C. B., *Simon Wilkin of Norwich* (1979)

Lewis, C., *Great Yarmouth, History, Herrings and Holidays* (1980)

Meeres, F., *A History of Norwich* (1998)

Nobbs, G., *Norwich: A City of Centuries* (1971)

*The Norfolk Pillar* (Norfolk Museums Service Information Sheet) (1977)

Norwich Castle Museum, *The Norfolk and Norwich Hospital* (1971)

Pigot & Co., J., *National Commercial Directory* (1830)

Pipe, C., *The Story of Cromer Pier* (1998)

Preston, J., *The Picture of Yarmouth* (1819)

Rawcliffe, C. and Wilson, R., *Norwich Since 1550* (2004)

Rounce and Wortley, *The History of the Cromer Lifeboats* (1939)

Rye, W., *Norfolk Families* (1913)

Savin, A. C., *History of Cromer* (1937)

Scott, C., *Poppyland* (1886)

Stibbons, P., Lee, K., & Warren, M., *Crabs and Shannocks: The Longshore Fishermen of North Norfolk* (1983)

Turner, *List of Norfolk Benefices* (1847)

Ward, C., *The Cottage on the Cliff: a Seaside Story* (1823)

Warren, M. *Cromer: the Chronicle of a Watering Place* (1994)

West Carnie, T., *In Quaint East Anglia* (1899)

White, W., *History, Gazetteer, and Directory of Norfolk* (1836)

Wilkin, M., *Joseph Kinghorn of Norwich* (1853)

## General

*Annual Register* (1825)

Blackburn, G., *The Illustrated Encyclopaedia of Ships, Boats, Vessels, etc.* (1978)

Carmen, W. Y., *A History of Firearms (1955)*

Curwen, J. S., *Old Plaistow* (1994)

Dale, R. W., *Manual of Congregational Principles* (1884)

Dalzall, W. R., *The Shell Guide to the History of London* (1981)

*Dictionary of National Biography*

Ebel, S., and Impey, D., *London's Riverside* (1975)

Greenhill, B., and Giffard, A., *Victorian and Edwardian Steamships from Old Photographs* (1979)

Jackson, D., *Lighthouses of England and Wales* (1975)

Keen, H., Jarrett, J., Levy, A., *Triumphs of Medicine* (1976)

Kent, A., *An Encyclopaedia of London* (1970)

Locke, D., *Virus Diseases* (1978)

Macdougall, P., *Royal Dockyards* (1982)

McNeill, W. M., *Plagues and Peoples* (1976)

Partner, R., *The Record of a Century 1807–1907*

Vernon Gibbs, C. R., *British Passenger Liners of the Five Oceans* (1963)

Ware, D., *A Short Dictionary of British Architects* (1967)

Weinreb, B., and Hibbert, C., *The London Encyclopaedia* (1993)

*Who Was Who*, Vol. IV (1952)

Willis, S. A., *Plaistow Congregational Church 1807–1957* (1957)

# Index

Lightning Source UK Ltd.
Milton Keynes UK
UKOW01f1523040318

318838UK00004B/103/P